AUSTIN A30 & A35

Kim Henson

CONTENTS

Foulis

Haynes

ISBN 0 85429 469 4

A FOULIS Motoring Book

First published 1985

© **Haynes Publishing Group**

Published by:
Haynes Publishing Group
Sparkford, Nr Yeovil,
Somerset BA22 7JJ

Haynes Publications Inc.
861 Lawrence Drive, Newbury
Park, California 91320, USA

Jacket colour illustration: This
Speedwell Blue two door A35 was
found derelict in a London suburb in
1981. It was restored by David
Clark, and now features 1275cc of
Austin Healey Sprite-power, yet
looks standard and very pretty
Photographs: Andrew Morland
Road tests: Courtesy of Motor and
Autocar
Printed in England by:
J.H. Haynes & Co. Ltd

Further titles in this series will be published at
regular intervals. For information on new titles
please contact your bookseller or write to the
publisher.

FOREWORD

The Austins A30 and A35 have always been popular cars. Today they still have a strong following, and are held in high regard for their cheeky, chubby looks and of course for their deeper, more important characteristics.

For example, their smoothness of running, mechanical simplicity, reliability, economy, durability and carrying capacity are all legend. Anyone who has been acquainted with an A30 or A35 for any length of time will confirm that these cars constantly amaze even their owners by the way they tackle any task put to them.

The styling is unusual, although of course in keeping with the Austin 'family look' of the early 'fifties, and is difficult to pigeonhole with any particular motoring era. To many enthusiasts it has become a symbol of good quality British engineering.

This 'Super Profile' is necessarily a compact volume. However, it encompasses a great deal of information about the Austin A30 and A35, hopefully giving a colourful picture of how the car developed and how it gained its considerable appeal.

From the 'History' chapter, through the sections covering production and technical details, road tests, owners' interviews, specialist services and books, to the photo gallery showing various aspects of the different models, there is plenty of information which I hope will encourage, entertain and enlighten anyone interested in these cars.

Acknowledgements

I should like to thank all those who have helped me in preparing this book.

Firstly, I must mention the many individual members of the Austin A30/A35 Owners' Club who helped me in various different ways. Some kindly allowed me to quiz them about their cars, and several permitted their vehicles to be photographed – often at considerable inconvenience to themselves. Just one such person was David Clark, who gave up his lunch in order that we could photograph his car before the weather changed.

Particular thanks in this respect must go to Norman Dobson, organizer of the A30/A35 Owners' Club Southern Counties Rally at Chichester, where many of the photographs for this book were taken. His helpfulness and forbearance in assisting with my numerous requests on the day of the Rally are greatly appreciated.

My thanks are due also to the many other A30 and A35 owners who so willingly helped me in my research and investigations for the book.

I am very grateful to Anders Clausager, of the British Motor Industry Heritage Trust, for his help, and particularly for permission to use copyright material relating to production figures.

For great assistance on the same subject I am also indebted to those at Austin Rover Group who provided some fascinating information.

My thanks to the managements of *Motor* and *Autocar* magazines, for their kind permission to reproduce their copyright road test articles, adding another dimension to the character descriptions of the cars.

I should like to thank Mr. Peter Brockes and his staff at the B.P. Library of Motoring, at Beaulieu, for their patience and helpfulness in dealing with my research. In addition, thanks must go to the National Motor Museum, Beaulieu, and to L.A.T. Photographic, for their permission to reproduce photographs of the A30 and A35 in action in motor sport.

Grateful acknowledgement as well to Andrew Morland who took the rest of the photographs.

I am indebted to the managements of MOTOR SPORT and *Motoring News* for channelling my enquiries in the right directions.

I am also grateful to Steve Gilks, who founded the A30/A35 Owners' Club, and who did much to fire my early enthusiasm for the cars.

Last, but not least, I must thank my parents, who put up with my passion for old Austins until at length I married and moved away, taking my A30/35s and all their spare bits and pieces with me; and Elaine, my wife. She has not only gained the said cars and their parts, but has also been a great help in my research, sorting out documents, photographs and so on.

To all these people, I say a big 'Thank you'.

Kim Henson

Family tree

Post-war Britain was hungry for cars and in an effort to satisfy demand, most manufacturers started their production lines rolling again by re-introducing models that had been built before the war.

Austin were no exception to this, and so, by late 1945, their 'Eight' and 'Ten' models were again being built for civilian use (in fact, a further 33,000 Eights alone were produced in the following two years).

These cars, introduced in 1939, had several interesting features. The Eight replaced the 'Big Seven' (in actual fact itself an 'Eight' in terms of R.A.C. horsepower rating) and the ubiquitous 'Ruby' Seven, and had more modern, rounded lines, a one-piece 'alligator' bonnet and a 'platform' chassis. The Ten incorporated similar advanced thinking, taking the place of the much loved 'Cambridge' Ten.

However comfortable, rugged and reliable these cars were, there was little doubt that they were getting a little old-fashioned by the late 'forties.

Both cars had sidevalve engines of Pre-war design, and the styling, while neat, was hardly modern.

Changes were on the way in Austin's range, however, and their 'Sixteen' saloon of the late 1940s, while retaining the basic styling of the Eight and Ten (interestingly combined with a conventional chassis) was fitted with an overhead valve engine – a four-cylinder, 2.2-litre unit.

The Sixteen was the first Austin passenger car to have an overhead valve engine, and as such it was to start a trend ...

The same engine went on to power the A70 'Hampshire' and 'Hereford' models, producing 68bhp to earn the '70' designation.

These large cars were fitted with smoother, more rounded bodies than their predecessors, although still used a full traditional chassis.

A smaller (1200cc) overhead valve engine was also produced; this was a short-stroke type, like the 2.2-litre engine, now that the R.A.C. rating 'horsepower' tax (dictating small bore, long-stroke designs) had at last been abolished in Britain.

This 1200cc engine powered the A40 – a smaller version, in looks and character, of the A70 – from the end of 1947. This medium-sized family car, with its 42bhp, respectable performance, and independent front suspension, was the first British all-new, mass-produced car to appear after the war.

With governmental policy dictating export priority for car manufacturers (by limiting allocations of steel according to overseas sales levels), Austin sold many A40s abroad, supplying world markets as eager as our own to buy new cars.

This situation continued into the early 'fifties, with four cars being exported for every one sold in Britain.

The Austins of the day were fairly advanced when compared to the competition. For example, Ford were soldiering on with sidevalve engines (albeit reliable), transverse springing and pre-war body designs, while even Morris, with their revolutionary Issigonis-inspired Minor, were still using the 918cc sidevalve engine from the old Morris Eight.

However advanced Austins were technically, the firm was aware that it had no really small car with which to compete in world or home markets, although it was, of course, well represented in the medium and large car sectors.

Concept

Enter the A30 'Seven'.

Austin needed another Austin Seven, the car which had worked such wonders for them in the 'twenties and 'thirties.

Car makers abroad had built cars very obviously down to the lowest possible price, to provide cheap transport, albeit austere, for the public.

Austin, on the other hand, felt that it would be preferable to build a smaller version of their already successful family cars, with the aim of providing comfortable accommodation for four people, plus their luggage. This was to be achieved without sacrifice in handling, power, or smoothness, yet built at the lowest cost possible consistent with meeting these aims.

It was felt, too, that such criteria would help the car in its export markets, where for several years customers had been obliged to accept deficiencies in one or more of these areas, in order to get mobile at all.

Therefore, despite considerations of front wheel drive layouts, rubber suspension, two cylinder (and two stroke) engines, air cooling and so on, the design team finally settled on what was in fact a scaled down version of the A40.

Original designs for the A30 body by Holden Koto were pretty, but a shortened version, re-styled by Dick Burzi, at Longbridge, was the car accepted by management as being sufficiently 'Austin family' in its appearance.

The 'A30 Seven', as it was originally designated, shared approximately the same interior dimensions with its famous predecessor the 'Ruby' Seven, although the similarity ended there, as the new car was constructed in a totally different way.

Design

The A30 was the first Austin built on the unitary construction principle, with no separable chassis. The body unit was built in such a way that it was effectively a rigid box reinforced at strategic points for the attachment of the engine, transmission and suspension/steering assemblies.

With this integral construction, the car could be built cheaply, yet at the same time be rigid and comparatively light in weight.

A plus feature of the new car was that it was a four door saloon, at a time when most other small cars sported only two; also it was endowed with a large luggage boot at the rear, enclosed and accessible from outside the car, without having to disturb rear seat occupants.

Mechanically, the car was conventional in layout, with the front-mounted in-line engine driving the rear wheels.

At a time when other manufacturers like Ford were still using sidevalve engines and three-speed gearboxes, Austin equipped their new 'baby' car with a four-speed gearbox and an overhead valve engine. This unit, with a bore and stroke ratio the same as the larger A40 Devon and Dorset engine, gave three-quarters the power from two thirds the capacity of the A40 unit. Its 800cc produced 28 bhp, which gave the car a good power to weight ratio, and

endowed it with lively acceleration for the time.

It is this engine, designed by W.V. Appleby, and later known as the 'A-Series' BMC unit which, in updated form, is still to be found powering new BL cars in the mid-eighties.

The A-Series engine has been produced with many different capacities over the years. It powered the A30, A35, A40 Farina, Morris Minor and 1000, the Mini, 1100s, 1300s, Morris Marina, Austin Healey Sprites and MG Midgets, and Austins Allegro, Metro, Maestro and Montego.

The power from the compact engine of the A30 was transmitted through a four speed gearbox (with synchromesh on 2nd, 3rd and Top gears) and then via an open propeller shaft and threequarter floating rear axle to the rear wheels. The rear axle was attached to the body by semi-elliptic springs. These were allied with lever arm shock absorbers and an anti-roll bar.

At the front of the car, suspension was independent, with coil springs, wishbones and lever arm shock absorbers which also formed the upper suspension link. This system was employed on BL cars into the 80s, with the MG Midget.

The A30 steering was by cam and lever (or worm and nut) steering box and idler, with the wheels turning about swivel pins, and connected to the box by draglinks.

The Lockheed brakes were twin leading shoe, fully hydraulic at the front, with a hydro-mechanical linkage at the rear, operated from a single slave cylinder under the centre of the car.

Pressed steel, 13 inch roadwheels were used, fitted with 5.20 x 13 tyres; these were rather small by the standards of the time even for a car of modest dimensions, and helped to give the A30 a modern appearance.

Another advanced feature, for a small car, was the use of 12 volt electrics.

Production prototypes and testing

Prototypes of the new car were built in the Experimental Department at Longbridge, Birmingham. They were extensively tested in this country and, later, abroad.

Specific aspects of the vehicle, including suspension, were tested at the Motor Industry Research Association test track near Nuneaton, in Warwickshire, while many miles of normal road work accrued during extended tests on all types of road, and in all kinds of terrain in Britain.

Long-distance endurance evaluation also took place on the Continent, and, as a result, many minor modifications were made to the car prior to production commencing. These included, for example, changing the method of road wheel attachment from bolts to conventional stud and nut fixing.

Tooling and production

Since the A30 was of unitary construction, unlike previous Austin models, building the cars meant a rather different approach.

There were few components common with other models (apart from electrical ancillaries and a gearbox which bore some resemblance to the Austin Eight unit), so tooling for the new A30 Seven was largely new and unique.

The car was built alongside its A40 and A70 'big brothers', in a new assembly building, opened in 1951.

With fast-moving assembly tracks, the cars were completed quickly, and once the bodyshells were finished, the mechanical components could be added swiftly.

This was aided by good stock control and efficient supply of parts to the production line as they were needed.

As the bodyshells could be fitted with right or left-hand drive components at will, selection of export models was simplified; some cars were also produced in 'kit' form for assembly abroad.

Launch and promotion

The A30 Seven was unveiled to an eager press on 16 October 1951, with the public unveiling occurring a day later, at the Earls Court Motor Show for that year.

The small Austin was a great attraction, taking pride of place on the Austin stand, where a partially sectioned vehicle was on display to show off the amount of interior room. The engine and gearbox were also sectioned to show mechanical detail to an interested public.

Austin promoted the car from several angles. In the first place, they were anxious to link the new car with its famous ancestor, the Austin Seven, and the same name was used initially. Comparisons were therefore made in advertising literature, equating the economical running, reliability and comparative roominess of the A30 with the well known and loved pre-war Seven.

At the same time, Austin publicity was quick to point out the significant strides in design made since the famous old Seven ceased production in 1939.

For example, the new car's overhead valve engine, independent front suspension, four doors, and large luggage compartment all received coverage in Austin's promotional material.

'Motoring with money in your pocket' was one slogan which Austin used to promote the A30. To underline this message, the economies of buying, running and maintaining (through long-lasting, dependable components) an A30 were fully stressed. In addition, the benefits of the car's small size (for instance it was the narrowest on

the British market at the time) were also well documented in terms of handiness for parking and garaging.

The efficiency of the engine was promoted, with particular regard to the use of an overhead valve layout; emphasis also being placed on the quietness and smoothness of the four-cylinder engine.

The 12 volt electrical system was brought to the attention of potential buyers, and also the advanced 'Roto-dip' bodywork preparation prior to painting. This system was a 'revolving spit' treatment for each bodyshell which gave them a phosphate coating to reduce the corrosion effects of localised damage. This coating was then followed by priming and baking, before the top coats were applied.

Such treatment was very advanced in the early 'fifties, and Austin were keen to bring such innovation to the attention of potential purchasers.

Public reaction

Both press and public were keen to examine the new Austin, and having done so, were enthusiastic in their praise for the car.

At a time when most motorists were still driving cars of pre-war design, the innovative A30 held many attractions. In particular, the lively overhead valve engine driving through a four-speed gearbox gave good performance and economy. Motoring journalists of the time also spoke of the good ride and reasonably taut handling compared with most small cars, this in part due to the new independent front suspension.

Members of the car-buying public were also appreciative of these aspects of the new car's character.

Another important point in the A30's favour was that, while being built very much with production costs and selling price in

mind, it was still well-finished, and in no way austere. While there were no frills, the Austin was tastefully furnished and pleasant.

To a public eager to buy 'modern' small cars, the A30 had a great deal to offer.

Contemporary competitors

At the time of the A30's introduction, there were few small cars available on the British market.

The Ford Anglia 'Eight' and the sidevalve Morris Minor were popular cars, and the Minor was fitted with the A30 engine following the merger of Austin and Morris to form B.M.C. (British Motor Corporation) in 1952. This brought the Minor and A30 into more direct competition, since the Morris now had an overhead valve engine.

To put the cars into perspective, the price of the A30 in January 1953 was £504 including tax, compared with £445 for the Anglia, and £530 for the (ohv) Minor. Another car in this market was the Renault 750, but at £610 it was fairly expensive at the time.

Soon, more new cars became available in Britain, notably the directly comparable Standard 'New Eight'. This car, with similar accommodation (apart from an 'internal' luggage boot) had an engine of identical bore, stroke, capacity and power output to the A30, although the design was rather different. At its introduction in September 1953, the new Standard sold for £481 in basic form, and was obviously aimed at the same potential buyers as the Austin.

Other contenders to arrive shortly afterwards were three new Fords and a Fiat. The Fiat 500, available here in Britain from July 1954, was quite expensive for a tiny car at £573.

The Fords, introduced in late 1953, were not expensive and

were therefore very serious contenders in the UK small car market.

The New Anglia and Prefect were two and four door saloons, respectively, with neat styling. They still had sidevalve engines (1172cc) and three-speed gearboxes, but were attractive cars, and a little larger than the A30. The Anglia sold for £511, and the Prefect for £526.

Ford's 'upright' tradition was continued, however, with the new Popular (103E). Looking very much like its predecessor, the Anglia Eight, the 'Pop' had a sidevalve 'Ten horsepower' engine, also of 1172cc. It was old-fashioned, with transverse leaf springing, three-speed gearbox and so on, and it was very basic. However it provided cheap, reliable no-nonsense motoring, and with a price tag of only £391 it appealed to many.

Of all these vehicles, only the Minor was perhaps more technically advanced than the A30. With torsion bar front suspension and rack and pinion steering, the Minor handled well, and had more room inside. However, with its original sidevalve engine it was rather underpowered: a problem greatly reduced by fitting the A30 engine.

So the A30 was an up to date design and competitive in price, considering its specification. However, it was joined by a number of cars from other makers, all keen to take a slice of the small car market, as the 1950s progressed. The introduction of the A35, in 1956, kept Austin in the lead, as described in the next Section.

Production evolution

The general concept of the A30/35 remained unchanged throughout its production life; that is to say a small, economical car but encompassing as far as possible big car comforts.

Changes to the original car were mainly minor ones, but all were worthwhile and some made significant contributions towards keeping the vehicle up to date and attractive to the buying public.

The first major alterations to the A30 were announced in October 1953, when, for the first time, a two door version was made available. This shared the same overall dimensions as the earlier version, but the doors were much wider than the front ones on the four door cars. The aim was to provide easier access for front seat passengers. Getting in or out of the rear compartment was not very much more difficult since both front seats tipped, and the passenger seat was 'double-jointed', the backrest folding forward onto the seat base, and the whole tilting forward to give unimpeded access.

On both two and four door cars, the dashboard was new, with a full-width parcel shelf below (previously there were two small 'cubby holes' at each side of the central, round speedometer).

In addition, the boot area was completely redesigned. The spare wheel, previously stowed immediately behind the rear seat, was now mounted upright on the nearside of the luggage compartment, and sunk into a well in the floor. At the same time, the fuel tank was changed, with the filler pipe now entering from the rear panel of the car, instead of from the offside rear wing.

External boot hinges, rather than the internal cantilever system previously used, were also fitted.

The effect of these two changes was to increase the useable amount of boot space.

Modifications were also made to the seats, to improve interior room, and to door trims and handles, neatening the appearance of the car from inside. On the outside, the grille size was increased, and the winged Austin badge disappeared.

For 1955, van and 'Countryman' (an Austin term for estate car) versions became available.

The most significant changes in the history of the car came in September 1956, however.

Most important was the increase in engine capacity to 948cc, resulting in raised power output of 34bhp and earning the car its new brake horsepower-related title of 'A35'.

Although the engine was of the same basic design as the earlier 803cc unit, many detail design changes were effected. These made the unit more powerful and longer-lasting. High speed tests on German *autobahnen* proved that lead/indium lined bearing shells stood up far better at sustained high engine speeds than the white metal lined type previously used, and so the new shells were used in the modified engine. A 'full flow' oil filter was also fitted, in place of the bypass type used on the A30.

Taking into account the new availability of 'Premium' petrol, the compression ratio was raised from 7.2 to 8.3:1, and this, combined with an increase in bore size, gave the engine its 34bhp compared with the 803cc unit's output of 28bhp.

At the same time, the gear ratios were revised to provide more even spacing, and a remote control gearchange with a short gearlever was incorporated.

The rear axle ratio, already raised twice in the early days of A30 production, was lifted again. This gave the car a more comfortable cruising ability at speed.

Flashing indicators were now fitted instead of the semaphore type on earlier cars, and the grille panel was now painted and encased in a chrome surround, in place of the all-chrome panel used previously.

The appearance of the car was also altered by enlarging the back window (it now 'wrapped around' slightly), and by changing the roof drain channel. This now followed the door pillar line, down to the front wing tops, instead of running across the top of the windscreen, as on the A30.

The interior was similar, but the A35 had different front seats and the speedometer was calibrated to 80mph (previously 70mph).

The A35 saloons continued, in two and four door form, basically unchanged until production ceased in 1959, although alterations were made to the commercial models.

For a brief period – 1956 and 57 only – a Pick-up version of the A35 was available. This was a pretty vehicle, and much more luxurious than the average utility, having a grabrail and outside step for occasional rear compartment passengers.

The vans and Countryman continued after discontinuation of the saloons, and until 1962 they used the 948cc engine.

Changes announced in April of that year gave the vehicle new side doors (plain, without recessed panels as previously), a white painted grille and wheels, and a bright-plated body moulding: this was the 'Mark II' version.

However, in October 1962, a 'Mark III' was announced, with the BMC 1098cc A-series engine and the Countryman was discontinued. To cope with the increased payload (6cwt instead of 5cwt previously), the 45bhp engine drove through a larger diameter, heavy duty clutch to a stronger gearbox, and to the rear wheels via a higher ratio axle.

From September 1964, the 848cc Mini size engine was used in some vans, mated to the same gearbox as employed on the 1098 model, but with a lower axle ratio. The 848cc engine produced 34bhp (the same as the 948cc unit) by using an SU carburettor. The 848 and 1098 vans were built side-by-side until the larger-engined model was discontinued in May 1966.

The last A35 (848cc) was built in February 1968.

Motorsport

When the A30 was introduced, there was some concern that its 800cc engine size would prevent competitive participation in international sporting events, since it was outside the 750cc class.

However, the A30 did get used a great deal for various forms of motorsport, from events such as the Lands End and Exeter Trials to International Rallies. The car proved popular in racing, timed driving tests and rallies, where it competed well against opposition such as Standard Eights and Morris Minors. Its manoeuvrability and reliability made it a good choice.

Perhaps the most famous of A30 competition victories was an outright win for Raymond Brookes and his father in the 1956 Tulip Rally, beating Standard Eights into the next three places.

With the introduction of the A35, competition potential was increased dramatically. The stronger 948cc engine was eminently tunable to give surprising performance, but even in standard form, the car was lively enough to partake successfully in motor sport.

To prove the point, a standard (with the exception of extra instruments and a higher back axle ratio) A35 two door saloon lapped Montlhery circuit, in France, for seven days and nights at an average speed of 74.9mph! The drivers, all Cambridge undergraduates under the leadership of Gyde Horrocks, took seven International class 'G' records in the process, and the car ran well throughout.

By fitting an anti-roll bar at the front, and *removing* the production anti-roll bar at the rear, the cars could be made to handle much better, and with breathing modifications, an A35 could show a clean pair of heels to many potentially faster vehicles.

Drivers like Graham Hill, with his famous car 69 PMT, John Sprinzel, Dickie Barrett and so on,

made motoring headlines throughout the late 'fifties and early 'sixties with a string of class and outright wins, mainly in circuit racing.

The A35 was a good rally car too, and competed against more modern machinery until comparatively recently – scoring a class win in the 1973 Welsh Rally, for example.

The competitive days of A35 driving are not over yet, however, and the car has been particularly successful in Classic Saloon Car racing in recent years, where it does battle with contemporary Morris 1000s, Standard Tens, MG Magnettes, Jaguars, Borgwards and many others.

It is a tribute to the original design of the car, and its inherent strength and reliability, that A35s are still highly competitive machines.

End of the road

The A35 sold well throughout its production life, as did the A30 before it.

However, by the late 'fifties public taste was changing and Austin planned a 'new look' range for the 1959 model year. This included the Farina-inspired, angular bodywork which was to be the hallmark of BMC cars for the following years. At the same time, the revolutionary front wheel drive Mini (also called an 'Austin Seven' initially) became BMC's smallest car.

The new A40 Farina, announced in late 1958, was really the successor to the A35 with virtually identical mechanical components: this car continued, with revisions, until 1967.

However the combined effects of the new styling and configuration of the A40 and Mini respectively sadly rendered the A35 obsolete.

The last A30 was produced in September 1956, and the last A35 saloon was finished less than three years later, in August 1959. The commercial models carried on through the next nine years though, with the Countryman being discontinued in September 1962, and the last van built in February 1968 – more than sixteen years after the Press introduction of the original A30.

Commercial success

Both the A30 and the A35 were successful cars. Initial reaction to the A30 was favourable, and this was partly due to the solid reputation that the Austin Motor Company had established in earlier years. The public felt – and expected – that the A30 would be a reliable and competent vehicle, and the Austin-inspired saying 'one bought a car, but invested in an Austin' was taken seriously.

People were not disappointed, and the little Austin did most things very capably. While not a sports car, it was a good cruiser, provided cheap to run, comfortable family transport, and could be parked and housed in very small spaces.

The A35, with its more powerful engine and higher gearing, was an improved version in many ways, yet appealed to the same market, where it carved itself a reputation for dependability, economy and practicality.

The A30 was sold in quantity abroad, 71,220 of the total 222,823 built being exported (including commercials). This little car therefore helped Britain's export drive considerably in the early 1950s.

Of the total saloon car production of A30s, 190,353 in all, 65,260 (34%) were sent overseas and earned much needed money for Britain.

Unfortunately no exact export figures exist for the A35 models, but considerable numbers were sold abroad and it is known that, for example, half of the Pick-up production was exported.

For markets such as the United States, the A30 and A35 were rather slow and under-powered compared with the huge gas-guzzlers which were the American norm. With gasoline freely available and cheap, a small economy car was a little out of place, although some cars still found homes across the Atlantic, in America and Canada.

Many others went to Australia (mainly A30s), New Zealand, South Africa, France, Holland, Germany, Italy, Portugal, Malta and so on. Examples still survive in all these countries today.

TOTAL PRODUCTION

It is interesting to compare the production figures for the two cars, which were:

	A30	A35
2 door Saloon	94,894	105,751
4 door Saloon	95,459	31,246
Van	26,047	210,575
Countryman	6,423	5,780
Pick-up	–	497
TOTAL	222,823	353,849

This gives a combined figure of 576,672.

EVOLUTION

Particular models of the A30/35 are easily identified by reference to **the vehicle identification plate.** This can be found under the bonnet, on the offside of the bulkhead or wing area on early cars, and on the front passenger door pillar on later vehicles.

This plate contains the car number, and is prefixed by the model identification code – in the case of left-hand drive vehicles, an 'L' is an additional prefix letter in the code.

Under this system, 'A' indicates the engine type (A-series), 'S' stands for four doors (and '2S' for two doors), 'P' for Countryman, 'V' for van, and 'K' for Pick-up. The model *series* number (3, 4, 5, 6, or 8) immediately follows the appropriate combination of letters.

The **engine number** is found on the top of the cylinder block, adjacent to the dynamo. Until August/September 1954, (chassis number 72037), the A30 had chassis and engine numbers which were different. From then until August 1959, engine and chassis numbers matched on each car – useful for identifying original engines.

On A35 models, the engine number is prefixed by another information code, under which the number indicates the engine size.

Therefore '9' equates to 948cc engines, '10' to 1098cc units, and '8' to the 848cc unit. 'AB' following this number simply means that the engine has Lucas electrical connections. The letter 'U' shows a central, floor gearchange, and the next letter, 'H' or 'L', prefixing the engine's number, indicates 'high' or 'low' compression.

Changes through the years

The first A30 (Series AS3), was introduced at the 1951 Earls Court Motor Show, although quantity production did not commence until May 1952. Originally called the 'Austin Seven', the name was amended to A30 shortly after the car's introduction, following the abolition of the infamous 'RAC horsepower' tax.

The car had an all-steel body of integral unitary construction, with the running gear attached directly to it, and with no separate chassis. Power came from a four-cylinder overhead valve engine, mounted in line with a four-speed gearbox (synchromesh on 2nd, 3rd and Top gears). Transmission was by open propeller shaft to the hypoid three quarter floating rear axle.

Only a four door body was available initially, with four seats and a large luggage boot. The dash panel incorporated a central, round speedometer and two open glove boxes. AS3 chassis numbers ran from 101 to 30602, and the model was produced until November, 1953. Significant production changes were:

1952 – From chassis number 1019, the axle ratio was raised from 5.143:1 to 5.125:1. From chassis number 1264, Unified threads replaced BSF type.

1953 – From October – for 1954 models – two and four door versions became available. On all cars the effective boot space was increased by fitting external hinges,

re-positioning the spare wheel on the left-hand side and moving the filler pipe for the fuel tank from the right-hand rear wing to the back panel.

Interior room was maximised by re-designing the seats and door panels, and a new facia with a full-width parcel shelf below was fitted. The (optional) heater was now an under-bonnet fitment, and to accommodate this the battery was moved to the right-hand side of the scuttle from its previously central position.

Two door models (A2S4) started at chassis number 25631, four door cars (AS4) from 25621.

1954 – The final drive ratio was raised to 4.875:1 on saloons, from chassis numbers 43898 (AS4) and 43849 (A2S4). From chassis number 70376, the cooling system was pressurised. From August, the 5cwt van (AV4) was built, starting at chassis number 68746, with the Countryman (AP4) from September, number 73987 onwards. The main differences over the saloons were the lower final drive ratio (5.375:1), roof air vent (vans only), stronger rear springs (11 leaves instead of 8), and larger tyres (5.60 x 13 instead of 5.20). In December, the valve adjustment screws were modified to improve security.

1955 – In May, tubeless tyres were made a standard fitting.

From June, hide seats were available as an option instead of leathercloth.

In July, manifold-driven automatic screen washers were available. Oil-filled ignition coils were now used.

From September (chassis number 139139) the Zenith 26JS carburettor was replaced by the 26VME type (with separate float chamber) to improve hot starting.

In October, moulded knobs on the starter and choke controls were fitted.

In December, the Countryman gained chrome mouldings and new weatherstrips for the rear and side windows.

The ball ends on the side and cross tubes were modified.

1956 – In January, the cylinder head was modified, and shorter exhaust valve guides were fitted (also fitted for inlet valves), to prolong the life of the valves when using leaded fuels.

From March, modified connecting rods were employed.

In May, the bonnet surround beading was discontinued, and larger ends were fitted to the gear selector fork rods. In September (for 1957 models), the most significant changes in the car's history took place.

The engine was enlarged to 948cc, with a compression ratio of 8.3:1 (formerly 7.2:1), lead-indium lined bearings (instead of white metal) and full-flow filtration (rather than the bypass system). The engine's power output was up by more than 21% at slightly lower revs than the 803cc unit. The final drive ratio was increased to 4.55:1, and the new gearbox had a remote control, short lever gearchange, more evenly spaced ratios and slicker operation.

The saloons had a larger, wrap-around back window and flashing indicators. Different seats were fitted, giving more rear seat legroom. The bonnet and doors were altered slightly, the change in door profile was to accommodate revised roof drain channels, which now ran down the front door pillars instead of across the top of the windscreen.

The A30's chrome grille was replaced by a painted panel, now having a thick chrome surround. De-luxe versions were available, with over-riders, opening rear side windows (two door cars), and twin ashtrays. Optional extras included a passenger's sun visor, a radio and a heater-demister unit.

The A35 Pick-up was introduced.

A35 chassis numbers commenced at 103 (A2S5), 112 (AS5), 204 (AV5), 329 (AK5) and 367 (AP5).

1957 – Pick-up production ceased in November (chassis number 78984).

1959 – Saloon production finished at chassis number 203929 (A2S5) and 203980 (AS5), in August. The vans continued in production; from chassis number 206001, engine and chassis numbers were no longer the same.

1962 – In February, production of the AV5 van and AP5 Countryman ceased at chassis numbers 282531 and 282005 respectively. Production of the Mark II A35, in van and Countryman forms only, commenced in February and March respectively, and ceased in September. The vans (AV6) started at chassis number 101 and finished at 13396, while the Countryman (AP6) ran from 2101 to 10954. Still with the 948cc engine, these vehicles had flashing indicators, white wheels and grille, plated body mouldings and plain door panels.

From September, a Mark III model was produced, in van form only (AV8). This had a 6cwt payload, a 1098cc version of the A-Series engine producing 45bhp and with a 7.5:1 compression ratio. The crankshaft bearings were steel-backed copper-lead, and carburation was now by an SU HS2 type unit.

A stronger gearbox, larger clutch and higher power driving through a 4.22:1 ratio axle, coped with the bigger payload. Windscreen washers were standard equipment.

Chassis numbers commenced at 13401.

1964 – An 848cc version of the Mk III van was introduced in September, using the Mini engine mounted conventionally and allied to the gearbox from the 1100 van, but with a 4.875:1 back axle (same ratio as later A30s). This version was initially produced alongside the 1100 van. Chassis numbers started at 47542.

1966 – Production of the 1100 van ceased at chassis number 62548, in May.

1968 – The 848cc version of the AV8 ceased in February, at chassis number 73315, marking 'the end of the line' for the A35.

SPECIFICATION

Specification Austin A30/A35

Built

Longbridge, Birmingham. (Commercial and Countryman bodies by Fisher and Ludlow, Castle Bromwich).

Type designation (including 'L' - left-hand drive models):

Saloon (A30)
AS3 – 4 door. Produced May 1952 to November 1953.
AS4 – 4 door. Produced October 1953 to September 1956.
A2S4 – 2 door. Produced October 1953 to September 1956.

Saloon (A35)
AS5 – 4 door. Produced September 1956 to August 1959.
A2S5 – 2 door. Produced September 1956 to August 1959.

Commercials (A30)
AV4 – 5cwt van. Produced August 1954 to September 1956.

Commercials (A35)
AV5 – 5cwt van. Produced September 1956 to February 1962.
AK5 – Pick-up. Produced September 1956 to November 1957.
Mark II, AV6 – 5cwt van. Produced February 1962 to September 1962.
Mark III, AV8 – 6cwt van (1098cc). Produced September 1962 to May 1966.
Mark III, AV8 – 6 cwt van (848cc). Produced September 1964 to February 1968.

Estate (A30)
AP4 – Countryman. Produced September 1954 to September 1956.

Estate (A35)
AP5 – Countryman. Produced September 1956 to February 1962.
Mark II, AP6 – Countryman. Produced March 1962 to September 1962.

Number built (A30)

A total of 222,823 A30s were built, of which 42.8% were 4 door saloons, 42.6% 2 door saloons, 11.7% vans, and 2.9% Countryman models. Specific production figures are shown at the end of the 'History' chapter.

Number built (A35)

A total of 353,849 A35s were built, of which 8.9% were 4 door saloons, 29.9% 2 door saloons, 59.5% vans, 1.6% Countryman models, and a tiny 0.14% were Pick-ups. Specific production figures are shown at the end of the 'History' chapter.

Total built (all models)

576,672

General configuration

Front engine, rear-wheel-drive through four-speed gearbox (synchromesh on second, third and top gears), open propeller shaft and three quarter floating hypoid rear axle.

Engine:

Type — Four-cylinders in-line, water-cooled. Pushrod-operated overhead valves and single camshaft in cast iron cylinder block. Cast iron cylinder head.

	A30	A35 (950)	A35 (1100)	A35 (850)
Capacity	803cc (49.0cu.in)	948cc (57.8cu.in)	1098cc (67.0cu.in)	848cc (51.7cu.in)
Compression ratio	7.2:1	8.3:1 (H.C.) 7.2:1 (L.C.)	8.5:1 (H.C.) 7.5:1 (L.C.)	8.3:1
Bore & stroke	58 x 76.2mm. (2.28 x 3.00in)	62.9 x 76.2mm. (2.48 x 3.00in)	64.6 x 83.7mm. (2.54 x 3.30in)	62.9 x 68.3mm. (2.48 x 2.69in)
Maximum bhp (net)	28 at 4800rpm	34 (H.C.), 32 (L.C.) at 4750rpm (H.C.), 4600rpm (L.C.)	48 (H.C.), 45 (L.C.) at 5100rpm	34 at 5500rpm
Maximum torque (lb/ft)	40 at 2200rpm	50 (H.C.), 48 (L.C.) at 2000rpm (H.C.), 2200rpm (L.C.)	60 (H.C.), 57 (L.C.) at 2500rpm (H.C.), 3000rpm (L.C.)	44 at 2900rpm
Carburettor	Zenith 26JS or 26VME	Zenith 26VME	SU HS2	SU HS2

Transmission:

	A30	A35 (950)	A35 (1100)	A35 (850)
Clutch (dia.)	6.25in	6.25in	7.25in	7.25in
Gear ratios:				
First	4.091:1	3.628:1	3.628:1	3.628:1
Second	2.591:1	2.374:1	2.172:1	2.172:1
Third	1.680:1	1.412:1	1.412:1	1.412:1
Top	1.000:1	1.000:1	1.000:1	1.000:1
Reverse	5.180:1	4.664:1	4.664:1	4.664:1
Final drive ratio	7/36=5.143:1 (*1) 8/41=5.125:1 (*2) 8/39=4.875:1 (*3) 8/43=5.375:1 (*4)	9/41=4.556:1	9/38=4.222:1	8/39=4.875:1
Overall ratios:				
First	21.040:1 (*1) 20.966:1 (*2) 19.944:1 (*3) 21.989:1 (*4)	16.529:1	15.317:1	17.687:1
Second	13.326:1 (*1) 13.279:1 (*2) 12.631:1 (*3) 13.927:1 (*4)	10.816:1	9.170:1	10.589:1
Third	8.640:1 (*1) 8.610:1 (*2) 8.190:1 (*3) 9.030:1 (*4)	6.433:1	5.961:1	6.884:1
Reverse	26.641:1 (*1) 26.548:1 (*2) 25.253:1 (*3) 27.843:1 (*4)	21.249:1	19.691:1	22.737:1

Notes: 1, A30–AS3 models to chassis no. 1018; 2, A30–AS3 models from chassis no. 1019 and early AS4/A2S4 models; 3, A30–AS4/A2S4 models from chassis no. 43898 and 43849 respectively; 4, A30–AV4/AP4 models.

Body construction — All steel, welded. Unitary bodyshell with reinforced mounting points for running gear and suspension.
Saloons, vans, estate cars and pick-up produced.

Dimensions:

Overall length	11ft. 4$\frac{3}{8}$in. (saloons); 11ft. 5$\frac{7}{8}$in. (commercials).
Overall width	4ft. 7$\frac{1}{8}$in. (saloons); 4ft. 8in. (commercials).
Overall height	4ft. 10$\frac{1}{4}$in. (A30 saloon); 4ft. 11$\frac{1}{4}$in. (A35 saloon); 5ft. 3in. (commercials).
Wheelbase	6ft. 7$\frac{1}{2}$in. (all models).
Track (front)	3ft. 9$\frac{1}{4}$in. (all models).
Track (rear)	3ft. 10$\frac{3}{4}$in. (all models).
Turning circle	35ft. (all models) between walls. 2$\frac{1}{3}$ turns lock-to-lock.
Ground clearance (min)	Minimum ground clearance 6$\frac{3}{8}$in. (saloons), 7in. (commercials).

Suspension:

Front	Coil springs with lower wishbone, allied to lever arm hydraulic shock absorbers which also form the upper suspension link. Independent.
Rear	Semi-elliptic leaf springs (saloons, eight leaves; commercials, eleven leaves), controlled by lever arm hydraulic shock absorbers and an anti-roll bar.

Steering   Steering box and idler system with track rod and side links to king pins. Worm and peg steering box unit by Cam Gears has 11:1 ratio; worm and nut unit by Burman (less common) has 12:1 ratio.

Brakes   Lockheed twin leading shoe, fully hydraulic at front, with hydro-mechanical operation at rear by single slave cylinder mounted under the floor of the car. Mechanical links connect the slave cylinder with the rear brake shoes via expander units in the brake drums, mounted on the rear backplates.

Wheels and tyres   Pressed steel wheels with ventilation slots; four stud holes.
Saloon tyres 5.20 x 13 crossply; Countryman and Commercial tyres 5.60 x 13 crossply (5.90 x 13 optional).

Kerb weight   Saloons, Vans and Pick-up, 14cwt. approx.; Countryman, 15cwt. approx.

Electrical system:

Type	Lucas, 12 volt, positive earth.
Battery	Capacity: 30 amp/hrs (A30); 38 amp/hrs (early A35); 43 amp/hrs (later A35).
Dynamo	Type: C39 PV2, output 19 amps (A30, early A35); C40-1, output 22 amps (later A35).
Lights	Headlamps: 42/36 watts (50/40 watts can be fitted).
	Sidelamps, number plate lamp: 6 watts.
	Stop/tail lights: 18/6 watts (21/6 watts can be fitted).
	Trafficators: 3 watts.
	Flashing indicators: 21 watts.
	Panel lamps: 2.2 watts.

Ignition system:

Type	Lucas, coil, distributor with contact breaker.
Distributor	Type: Lucas DM2 (A30 and 948cc A35); 25D4 (848 and 1098cc A35).
Coil	Type: Lucas Q12 (early A30); LA12 (other models).

Performance (saloons):	A30 (803cc)	A35 (948cc)
Max. speed (mph)	63	72
Speed in gears (mph):		
First	18	21
Second	27	34
Third	43	57
Acceleration from rest (seconds):		
0–30mph	8.0	6.6
0–40mph	14.2	11.8
0–50mph	23.0	17.8
0–60mph	38.5	29.2

	A30 (803cc)	**A35 (948cc)**
Standing Quarter mile (seconds)	25.8	23.5
Acceleration on the move (seconds):		
Third gear:		
20–40mph	10.5	8.4
30–50mph	–	11.3
Top gear:		
20–40mph	14.7	11.9
30–50mph	17.7	13.5
40–60mph	27.7	18.4
Fuel consumption (mpg):		
In town	38–40	36–40
Touring	40–45	42–48

ROAD TESTS

The Motor Road Test No. 16/52

Make: Austin **Type:** A30 Seven

Makers: The Austin Motor Co., Ltd., Longbridge, Birmingham

Dimensions and Seating

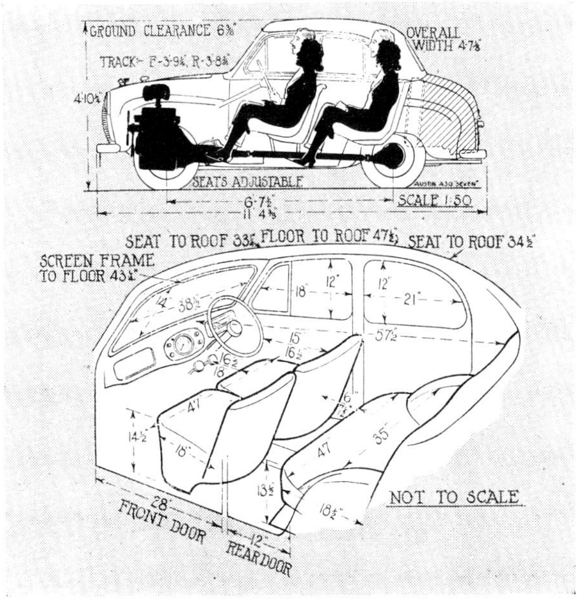
GROUND CLEARANCE 6⅜"
TRACK:- F-3-9¾, R-3-8¾
OVERALL WIDTH 4-7⅜
4-10¼"
SEATS ADJUSTABLE
AUSTIN A30 "SEVEN"
6-7½"
11 4⅜"
SCALE 1:50
SEAT TO ROOF 33½
FLOOR TO ROOF 47½
SEAT TO ROOF 34½"
SCREEN FRAME TO FLOOR 43½"
12"
18"
21"
38½
57½
15
16½
NOT TO SCALE
FRONT DOOR
REAR DOOR

Test Conditions

Weather; mild, with strong wind blowing along course. Surface; smooth tarmac, damp during most of tests. Fuel; Pool petrol.

Test Data

ACCELERATION TIMES on Two Upper Ratios

	Top	3rd
10-30 m.p.h.	15.5 secs.	8.4 secs.
20-40 m.p.h.	15.3 secs.	10.6 secs.
30-50 m.p.h.	19.9 secs.	—

ACCELERATION TIMES through gears

0-30 m.p.h.	8.5 secs.
0-40 m.p.h.	15.2 secs.
0-50 m.p.h.	29.0 secs.
Standing Quarter Mile	26.5 secs.

FUEL CONSUMPTION

52½ m.p.g. at constant 20 m.p.h.
50½ m.p.g. at constant 30 m.p.h.
46 m.p.g. at constant 40 m.p.h.
39 m.p.g. at constant 50 m.p.h.

Fuel consumption (at touring speeds) for 84 miles, 2 gallons, equals 42 m.p.g. Fuel consumption (driving hard) for 148.5 miles, 4 gallons, equals 37.1 m.p.g. Overall consumption for 232.5 miles, 6 gallons equals 38.8 m.p.g.

MAXIMUM SPEEDS

Flying Quarter Mile

Mean of four opposite runs	62.2 m.p.h.
Best time equals	64.7 m.p.h.

Speed in Gears

Max. speed in 3rd gear	45 m.p.h.
Max. speed in 2nd gear	28 m.p.h.

WEIGHT

Unladen kerb weight	13½ cwt.
Front/rear weight distribution	54/46
Weight laden as tested	17¼ cwt.

INSTRUMENTS

Speedometer at 30 m.p.h.	8% fast
Speedometer at 60 m.p.h.	6% fast
Distance recorder	2% fast

HILL CLIMBING (at steady speeds)

Max. top gear speed on 1 in 20	47 m.p.h.
Max. top gear speed on 1 in 15	39 m.p.h.
Max. gradient on top gear	1 in 12.7 (Tapley 175 lb./ton)
Max. gradient on 3rd gear	1 in 7.4 (Tapley 300 lb./ton)
Max. gradient on 2nd gear	1 in 5.8 (Tapley 380 lb./ton)

BRAKES at 30 m.p.h.

0.95 g retardation (= 31½ ft. stopping distance) with 100 lb. pedal pressure
0.73 g retardation (= 41½ ft. stopping distance) with 75 lb. pedal pressure
0.44 g retardation (= 68½ ft. stopping distance) with 50 lb. pedal pressure
0.18 g retardation (=167 ft. stopping distance) with 25 lb. pedal pressure

In Brief

Price £355 plus purchase tax £198 14s. 5d. equals £553 14s. 5d. (Extra for heater, £9 6s. 8d. and for radio £43 11s. 1d.—both including P.T.).

Capacity	803 c.c.
Unladen kerb weight	13½ cwt.
Fuel consumption	38.8 m.p.g.
Maximum speed	62.2 m.p.h.
Maximum speed on 1 in 20 gradient	47 m.p.h.
Maximum top gear gradient	1 in 12.7
Acceleration	
10-30 m.p.h. in top	15.5 secs.
0-50 m.p.h. through gears	29.0 secs.

Gearing
12.6 m.p.h. in top at 1,000 r.p.m. 63.4 m.p.h. at 2,500 ft. per min. piston speed.

Specification

Engine	
Cylinders	4
Bore	58 mm.
Stroke	76 mm.
Cubic capacity	803 c.c.
Piston area	16.35 sq. in.
Valves	Overhead (pushrod)
Compression ratio	7.2/1
Max. power	28 b.h.p.
at	4.800 r.p.m.
Piston speed at max. b.h.p.	2,400 ft. per min.
Carburetter	Zenith downdraught (26 JS)
Ignition	Coil
Sparking plugs	Champion NA8
Fuel pump	AC mechanical
Oil filter	AC by-pass
Transmission	
Clutch	6¼ in. Borg and Beck s.d.p.
Top gear (s/m)	5.14
3rd gear (s/m)	8.64
2nd gear (s/m)	13.32
1st gear	21.03
Propeller shaft	Hardy Spicer
Final drive	Hypoid bevel
Chassis	
Brakes	Lockheed hydraulic (2LS on front)
Brake drum diameter	7 ins.
Friction lining area	61.1 sq. in.
Suspension: Front	Independent (coil)
Rear	Semi-elliptic
Shock absorbers	Armstrong hydraulic
Tyres	5.20 × 13
Steering	
Steering gear	Cam and lever
Turning circle	35 feet
Turns of steering wheel, lock to lock	2⅓
Performance factors (at laden weight as tested)	
Piston area, sq. in. per ton	19.0
Brake lining area, sq. in. per ton	70.9
Specific displacement, litres per ton mile	2,220

Fully described in "The Motor," October 17, 1951.

Maintenance

Fuel tank: 5¾ gallons. **Sump:** 5 pints, S.A.E. 30 (summer), 20 (winter). **Gearbox:** 2⅓ pints, S.A.E. 40. **Rear axle:** 1⅝ pints, S.A.E. 90. **Steering gear:** S.A.E. 140 E.P. **Radiator:** 8½ pints (2 drain taps). **Chassis lubrication:** By oil gun every 500 miles to 15 points, every 2,000 miles to 4 points and every 10,000 miles to 3 points. **Ignition timing:** T.D.C. **Spark plug gap:** 0.017 in.-0.019 in. **Contact breaker gap:** 0.014 in.—0.016 in. **Valve timing:** Inlet opens 5° B.T.D.C. and closes 45° A.B.D.C. Exhaust opens 40° B.B.D.C. and closes 10° A.T.D.C. **Tappet clearances:** (Hot or cold) Inlet and exhaust 0.012 in. **Front wheel toe-in:** $\frac{1}{16}$ in. to ⅛ in. **Camber angle:** 1°. **Castor angle:** 3°. **Tyre pressures:** Front 20 lb., rear 20 lb. (with full load, front 20 lb., rear 23 lb.). **Brake fluid:** Lockheed. **Battery:** 12-volt, 32 amp/hrs. **Lamp bulbs:** Headlamps (home), 42/36-watt (Lucas No. 354); sidelamps, 6-watt (Lucas No. 989); stop and tail light, 18/6-watt (Lucas No. 361); panel and warning indicator lamps, 2.2-watt (Lucas No. 987); Trafficators, 3-watt (Lucas No. 256).

Ref. B/9/52

November 12, 1952   *THE MOTOR*

—The A30 AUSTIN Seven

Latest Longbridge Product Offers Excellent Combination of Economy, Comfort and Performance

IT was at the Motor Show of 1951 that full details of the post-war Austin Seven were first announced to the public; long before that, however, the Austin Motor Co. Ltd. had publicly made known their intention to produce such a model. Recently, examples of the

Closely resembling the larger A40 and A70 models, the new Austin Seven has a compact and pleasing appearance. The low build of the car makes it particularly easy to reach the engine and accessories through the top-opening bonnet. Noticeable here are the air cleaner, battery, and radio installation, and the lugs for removing the engine may be seen on top of the valve cover.

car have been leaving the production lines at Longbridge at a steadily-increasing tempo but, even now, comparatively few people outside the immediate trade circle have had an opportunity of sampling the car for themselves.

These facts, coupled with the unique reputation of the makers in respect of the original between-wars Austin Seven, made this new version one of the most eagerly-awaited cars that has ever been introduced in this country.

Recently we had an opportunity of putting a Seven through our usual road test drill, coupled with a more-than-usually extended amount of general use under very varied conditions; and it can be said right away that this new example of the Seven is a car which will exactly fill the bill for many thousands of motorists and potential car users, both in this country and overseas.

Its price (purchase tax apart) is modest; it is very economical, with a fuel consumption of rather over 40 m.p.g. under touring conditions; it offers a surprising combination of comfort and compactness, occupying minimum garage space, but still providing accommodation for four; it is in every way a very roadworthy little car; and its acceleration and speed capabilities are greater than a large proportion of its potential public will ever require and adequate to satisfy the demands of the user

whose A to B journey times are higher than those of most of his fellows - the more so in view of the modest width and good handling which enable traffic to be negotiated with unusual ease.

So much for the overall picture. It is now possible to be more specific.

The 803 c.c. four-cylinder o.h.v. engine follows the general Austin practice in layout and is an extremely willing little unit which couples a good power output with a degree of flexibility which is most attractive in a small engine. As the accompanying data panel will show, it propels the car at comfortably over the mile-a-minute mark when required and it reveals no signs of distress when driven flat-out for considerable periods.

As with most cars, its characteristics show to best advantage over certain portions of the range and this Austin model,

with the gearing adopted, is at its most pleasant from 25 m.p.h. to 50 m.p.h. Similarly 35 m.p.h. is a comfortable speed for tackling long hills in third gear, although, in fact, some 10 m.p.h. in excess of this is available before valve bounce places a definite check on further revs.

Thanks to the flexibility of the engine, the Seven will travel very comfortably at speeds even as low as 12 m.p.h. in top gear when trickling along in a slow traffic stream and third gear is correspondingly adequate at speeds down almost to a crawl. Under normal conditions second-gear starts can be effected with no excessive clutch slip.

42 Miles per Gallon

So far as economy is concerned, the constant-speed figures given in the accompanying panel provide an excellent clue to the potentialities in this direction, ranging from 39 m.p.g. at a steady 50 m.p.h. to 52½ m.p.g. at 20 m.p.h.

As for overall figures, the consumptions recorded in a series of tests naturally varied considerably according to the conditions and driving methods. Handled as a very large proportion of owners will drive such a car, i.e. at touring speeds mainly in the region of 30-40 m.p.h., the car proved capable of covering 84 miles on 2 gallons. Really hard driving, at the other extreme, showed a figure of 37 m.p.g.

The clutch calls for little comment, smooth operation needing no particular finesse and the amount of pedal travel being comparable with other small cars and, accordingly, requiring none of the delicacy demanded by the clutch of the original Austin Seven, with its very short effective travel. The gearbox offers an

A deep rear window gives good visibility, and the way in which the four forward-hinged doors are pressed to form part of the integral wing lines is clearly shown.

THE MOTOR   *November 12, 1952*

The A30 Austin Seven -   -   -   -   - Contd.

acceptable standard of quietness and the gear change, by means of a conveniently-placed central lever, is straightforward, although an improvement could certainly be made in the matter of engagement of both first and second gears when the car is stationary, a second try frequently being required before the gears will engage. The synchromesh cones do their job reasonably well otherwise, although unduly-hasty movement will produce a mild protest.

Handling qualities of the Austin Seven are most satisfying. Very little effort is required on the wheel, the response is quick and accurate and only 2⅓ turns of the wheel are required from lock to lock. These characteristics, combined with a very slight tendency to oversteer (which never assumes anything approaching disconcerting proportions) make for a car which is particularly easy to thread in and out of traffic, whilst retaining a very pleasant degree of road-worthiness when being driven fast in the open country. Rolling is almost entirely absent (a torsional anti-roll bar is fitted at the rear) and this feature is particularly praiseworthy in view of the modest track, whilst another good point is that, even on bad surfaces, practically no road reaction is felt on the steering wheel.

Good by any Standards

Suspension, especially in view of the short wheelbase and small wheels, is particularly good, the manufacturers having achieved a compromise in spring rates and damper settings which cuts out all trace of pitching and float, yet irons out road irregularities in a most comfortable fashion without any suspicion of harshness. Taken altogether, in fact, the handling and suspension qualities of this car can be classed as good by any standards and particularly good for a model of such compact dimensions, where the provision of roadworthiness and comfort offer very much more difficult problems for the designer. In this respect, incidentally, the Seven also earns good marks for its handling on wet roads. As with any car, it is possible to produce a slide by violent handling on a slippery surface, but the attractive point is that, despite its short wheelbase and narrow track, the A30 is particularly controllable under these conditions and can, by the ultra-enthusiastic, be held quite entertainingly in a four-wheel drift.

Recorded figures can be allowed to tell their own story with regard to the excellent brakes but it remains to add a word of praise for the substantial and effective pull-up hand-brake, conveniently located alongside the driver's seat, where it is both accessible and out of the way.

In the main, the controls can be classed as nicely placed, but could be made even better with a little attention to one or two quite minor defects. A tall driver, for example, finds the accelerator pedal slightly awkward to maintain in half-throttle position indefinitely as this involves a rather tiring ankle position. Similarly, the excellent idea of mounting the lighting switch and horn button on an

A radio and heater are optional fitments in the roomy driving compartment. Notable here are the two-spoke steering wheel, conveniently long gear lever and sturdy handbrake. Below is seen the wide rear seat, the wheel arches forming armrests at the sides.

arm extending from the steering column could be made even better if the arm were mounted higher up the column to avoid any need for removing the hand from the wheel. Another small point is that it is necessary to switch on to the full beam before reaching the dip position, instead of the switch following the logical sequence of side, dip and full-on.

Comfortable Seating

Apart from these small points the general driving position is very good, offering an excellent view of both front wings surmounted by their nicely-placed sidelamps; whilst, thanks to the use of well-shaped foam-rubber cushions, the seats themselves are quite outstandingly comfortable for a car of this size. Both cushion and squab give a degree of all-round support unusual to find in so small a car, and a simple three-position adjustment is provided. The back seats, too, earn praise for the good all-round support which they offer and, whilst knee room is naturally limited, this Austin Seven will very definitely carry four full-sized occupants in comfort.

Entry and exit are easy in the front and call for no particular contortions where the rear is concerned, although, in the latter case, an improvement could be effected by arranging for the doors to open a few degrees more. Other points about the body are a pleasing absence of wind noise (rain water gutters are not fitted to the

screen pillars) and a very good degree of all-round visibility.

Luggage accommodation is surprisingly good bearing in mind the overall size of the car and the top-opening rear boot is adequate for two quite large suitcases, together with a quantity of smaller baggage. Inside the car there are two useful cubby holes flanking the centre instrument panel, one of these being used for the radio control panel, when fitted. On the car tested both radio and a heater were fitted and the heater proved adequate to maintain the car at a very comfortable temperature, although its demisting qualities could hardly be considered adequate. By opening the two hinged ventilating panels in the front doors, however, misting-up did not prove a serious problem except in heavy rain. Provision for ventilation is also made in the rear doors where there are similar pivoted panels in the rear portions, the main sections of the windows being fixed. At the front, the windows are of the direct-operated drop type and the door locking catch is arranged to lock the windows both in fully closed position and also when opened very slightly to allow circulation of air if the car is parked in hot weather.

The equipment generally is simple but adequate, as one would expect on a car of this type and good marks must be given for the lighting system which is more than adequate. The rather unusual handles inside the four doors, however, which move one way to secure the counter-balanced window panes and the other to release the door catch, can easily open the door when it is intended simply to unlock the window. There are no markings to explain their dual function and they only escape classification as dangerous because the doors are hinged from their forward edges.

In short, this new Austin Seven is a model which provides just those features which are required by an increasingly large section of the motoring public to whom economy, handiness and modest demands on garage accommodation are essential, but who require a fully-fledged car which matches up with normal standards of refinement and smatters in no way of crude motor-cycle practice.

Neat and businesslike sums up the appearance of the Countryman. The shape of the body and door panels adds strength and helps to prevent drumming. A guttering extends round the extremity of the roof line

The *Autocar* ROAD TESTS

No. 1584:

AUSTIN A.30 COUNTRYMAN

A narrow track is useful in rural conditions; there is provision for a starting handle and the bumper gives very reasonable protection

THE estate car, station wagon or utility—call it what you will—is a familiar sight. Before the days of large luggage boots this type of body was more often seen in countries where the owner was accustomed to taking all his personal luggage with him—especially in Africa, India and lands where railways were few and far between. The estate car type of bodywork thus became very popular. In addition to having a greater load-carrying capacity than the normal saloon car the extra floor space proved very useful on long journeys where hotels were few, as it was possible to sleep under cover in comparative comfort.

Motorists all over the world have now discovered the advantages of this type of body and for some years manufacturers have been building them on a quantity production basis. One of the latest, and certainly among the cheapest, is the Austin A.30 Countryman. It is light in weight, economical and comfortable, but small enough to park in a space which would have to be ignored by the drivers of most vehicles.

The engine is the smallest of the Austin range. It is identical with that fitted in the A.30 saloon and, to enable it to deal with the extra load which the Countryman might be expected to take, the axle ratio is raised to 5.375 to 1 from the 4.88 to 1 of the saloon. To obtain data which would approximate to conditions of everyday use, the Countryman carried throughout the Road Test 3 cwt of ballast made up of six canvas bags each containing ½ cwt of gravel. Four of the bags were placed on the platform and the other two occupied the space behind the front seats.

This load did not appear to have a great deal of effect on the performance. The engine would pull away quite cheerfully in second gear from standstill and first was required only when moving off on a gradient. Fish Hill, near Broadway, was climbed easily in third, the laden weight being over one ton. This indicated that the A.30 Countryman should be capable of carrying its full load of five hundredweight in addition to the driver practically any-where on a made road.

A pleasant cruising speed on main roads was at an indi-cated 50 m.p.h. on the near-accurate speedometer, and it was not difficult to maintain average speeds approaching 35 m.p.h. in favourable road and traffic conditions. Driving hard through hilly country had the effect of making the petrol consumption fall to 36 m.p.g. from the remarkable figure of 48 m.p.g. which was recorded with the minimum use of the gears and keeping the speed below 40 m.p.h. The fuel tank has a capacity of 5¼ gallons and appears to require filling very infrequently. When it was necessary it was a rather slow procedure, as petrol blew back at any-thing over half-flow from an electric pump.

Adequate power was available immediately after the first start in the morning and little use of the choke was necessary. At all speeds the unit was noticeably smooth and it pulled well at low r.p.m. The maximum torque of 40 lb ft is developed at 2,200 r.p.m. Those drivers who prefer to change gear as little as possible would find the Countryman well suited to their method of driving though the gear change itself is an easy one, and the synchromesh on the top three gears is effective. First speed on the model tested was a little noisy and at times difficult to engage from rest; clutch action was light and take up smooth on full load.

An efficient braking system should be part of the equip-ment of all vehicles but this applies even more so to one such as the Countryman, which might be called upon to operate heavily loaded in hilly country, for a laden car on a gradient requires a considerably increased effort to bring it to a halt. The A.30 brakes were up to all that was required of them during the Road Test. Only a light pressure was needed for all normal braking and there was no sign of unevenness during the brake testing. The hand-brake held the laden vehicle on a steep gradient and the lever, placed by the right side of the driving seat, is easy to reach.

Steering and road-holding of this small Austin are good, although the effect of the three hundredweight of ballast was noticed if the car was driven fast round a corner. On a wet or slippery surface the back of the car would slide a little, but response to correction was immediate. There was good directional stability at speeds in the region of 60 m.p.h. on straight roads, and once the driver realized the fact that oversteer was introduced by a load carried

The single rear door is hung on strong hinges, and the handle is provided with a lock. Half of each side window slides in its frame

over and behind the rear axle he could drive accordingly.

The suspension gave a good ride over many different kinds of surface. Taken down a mild trials hill in the Cotswolds which had a deeply rutted surface, the Country-man caused no undue discomfort, and springing and spring dampers prevented any bottoming in spite of the rather heavy load. As this type of vehicle is often called upon to operate off the beaten track it is a pity that the petrol pipe near the tank and the pipeline for the rear brakes are both in rather vulnerable positions for cross-country motoring.

There is a good, if somewhat upright, driving position. The short bonnet, which slopes down between the front wings, enables the driver to see obstacles close to the car and the Countryman can be driven along narrow lanes and through gateways with confidence, and with room to spare in most cases. The large side windows help in manœuvring and make the car a very good choice for use in crowded streets. It was in these conditions that the flexible pull on the driving side door became a nuisance as it rubbed the driver's elbow. The pedals are widely spaced, and there is room for large feet in the driving compartment.

There is a maximum interior width of 3ft 10½in, with 2ft 10½in between the wheel arches, and with the back of the rear seat folded down there is a platform length of 4ft 5½in

The interior finish is practical but not austere. Each door has a flexible pull strap; door windows are opened by a finger grip at the top. Counter-weighting provides a smooth action and they remain set at any opening

Super Profile

By tipping up a front seat it is a simple matter to get into the rear compartment. The floor mats can be removed with ease for cleaning

Spare wheel and the tool kit are housed in a separate compartment. In this view the rear seat is erected, showing resultant space; the width of the door opening is just over 2ft 7in

AUSTIN A.30 COUNTRYMAN . . .

The twin windscreen wiper blades fitted as standard were appreciated, as a small car always seems to get its screen dirtier than a large one; the blades cleared a good area of the A.30's screen.

It was a pleasure to drive at night because of the excellent beam from the head lights. The main beam was more than adequate for the speed of the car and in the dipped position cyclists and pedestrians could be picked out easily in spite of oncoming traffic. The lights are controlled by a small switch which projects from the right side of the steering column, and is operated without removing the hand from the steering wheel.

There is a single-note horn operated by a push button in the centre of the wheel boss. Semaphore-type direction indicators are supplied and these have a switch on the facia. They are not self-cancelling, but there is a bright warning light in the switch. The instruments are well lit and there is no reflection in the screen. A small light under the panel comes on when either side door is opened, but there is no roof light behind the seats.

The interior is well finished in p.v.c.-coated fabric and the four seat cushions have foam rubber fillings; they are firm and comfortable. The front seats are adjustable for leg room, and although when the driving seat is right back, as for a tall driver, the space in the rear seat on that side is somewhat limited, there is good room in general for four adults. The back rests of the front seats tip up, and also the whole seat hinges forward. This greatly helps entry to the rear seats.

With the rear seat in use some of the space is taken up by the rear wheel arches, but these also serve as arm rests. The back rest of this seat has a good depth of upholstery. It is held upright by two small screwed hooks which engage in brackets fixed to the side of the body. Hinged behind and to the top of the back rest is the extension which folds down to make a continuous flat floor behind the front seats. The back rest is covered in fabric; this would be better if it were protected with metal rubbing strips as the p.v.c.-coated cloth could easily be torn by a heavy box or case. The main floor of the rear compartment is of widely ribbed pressed steel. When the back

Large bore flexible pipes lead from the heater, when fitted, to the demisting vents. Oil vapour from the rocker cover is fed to the carburettor air cleaner. As usual with B.M.C., the engine is fitted with lifting eyes

AUSTIN A.30 COUNTRYMAN . . .

rest is down the rear seat cushions are placed in the footwells behind the front seats.

The rear door opening is a useful width and, when open, the door does not protrude past the side of the body or obstruct the right-hand rear light at night. There is no draught sealing rubber round the frame; the two side doors have such a seal in addition to the rubber seal round the door itself.

The spare wheel is held down by a screw clamp in a separate compartment beneath the main floor. The wheel is easy to remove from the housing. The starting handle included in the tool kit also serves as the wheelnut brace and jack handle. The jack fits in sockets on either side of the car; it is necessary to have the door open when screwing up or down. There are nineteen lubrication points which require attention with an oil gun every 1,000 miles.

Fitted to the test car were a heater and demisting unit and a radio set, both of which form part of the optional extra equipment which can be supplied with the Countryman. The heater provided adequate comfort in all seats on days when the outside air temperature was near freezing point; it is in action quickly after a cold engine start. The rheostat-controlled fan is noisy, and the handles of the adjustable air vents of the heater have undesirable sharp corners.

The radio fits neatly in the right-hand side of the parcels shelf which extends across the car below the facia. An exterior driving mirror is fitted in a satisfactory position; interior fittings include a single sun vizor for the driver. There is no ashtray.

The bonnet is opened by operating the Austin motif. There is a safety catch, but the bonnet is not locked from inside the car. Most of the under-bonnet units are well placed for maintenance, the battery especially so.

AUSTIN A.30 COUNTRYMAN

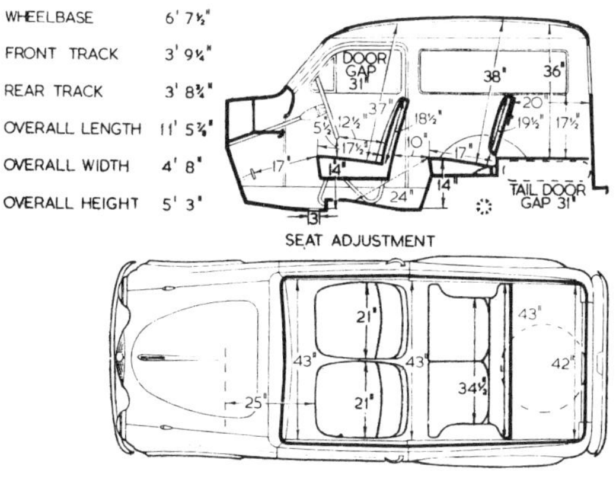
WHEELBASE 6' 7½"
FRONT TRACK 3' 9¼"
REAR TRACK 3' 8¾"
OVERALL LENGTH 11' 5¾"
OVERALL WIDTH 4' 8"
OVERALL HEIGHT 5' 3"
DOOR GAP 31"
TAIL DOOR GAP 31"
SEAT ADJUSTMENT

Measurements in these ¼in to 1ft scale body diagrams are taken with the driving seat in the central position of fore and aft adjustment and with the seat cushions uncompressed

PERFORMANCE

ACCELERATION: from constant speeds.
Speed Range, Gear Ratios and Time in Sec.

M.P.H.	5.375 to 1	9.03 to 1	13.921 to 1	21.984 to 1
10—30 ..	15.5	8.9	—	—
20—40 ..	16.5	11.8	—	—
30—50 ..	23.4	—	—	—

From rest through gears to:

M.P.H.	sec.
30	11.6
50	35.8

Standing quarter mile, 28.3 sec.

SPEEDS ON GEARS:

Gear		M.P.H (normal and max.)	K.P.H. (normal and max.)
Top ..	(mean)	59.3	95.4
	(best)	63.0	101.4
3rd		33—40	53—64
2nd		18—26	29—42
1st		12—16	19—26

TRACTIVE RESISTANCE: 35 lb per ton at 10 M.P.H.

TRACTIVE EFFORT:

	Pull (lb per ton)	Equivalent Gradient
Top	137	1 in 16.4
Third	242	1 in 9.2
Second	328	1 in 6.7

BRAKES:

Efficiency	Pedal Pressure (lb)
84.1 per cent	75
69.2 per cent	50
45.9 per cent	25

FUEL CONSUMPTION:
40.2 m.p.g. overall for 268 miles (7 litres per 100 km.).
Approximate normal range 36–48 m.p.g. (7.8–5.8 litres per 100 km.).
Fuel, first grade.

WEATHER: Sunny, slight breeze, dry surface.
Air temperature 48 deg. F.

Acceleration figures are the means of several runs in opposite directions.

Tractive effort and resistance obtained by Tapley meter.

SPEEDOMETER CORRECTION: M.P.H.

Car speedometer	10	20	30	40	50	60	65
True speed	10	19	28	38	48	58	63

DATA

PRICE (basic), with Countryman body, **£395.**
British purchase tax, **£198 17s.**
Total (in Great Britain), **£593 17s.**
Extras: Radio **£33.** Heater **£13 10s.**

ENGINE: Capacity: 803 c.c. (48.8 cu in).
Number of cylinders: 4.
Bore and stroke: 58 × 76 mm (2.28 × 3in).
Valve gear: overhead, push rods and rockers.
Compression ratio: 7.2 to 1.
B.H.P. 28 at 4,800 r.p.m. (B.H.P. per ton laden 25.9).
Torque: 40 lb ft at 2,200 r.p.m.
M.P.H. per 1,000 r.p.m. on top gear, 12.67.

WEIGHT: (with 5 gals fuel), 15 cwt 2 qtr (1,736 lb).
Weight distribution (per cent): F, 50; R, 50.
Laden as tested: 21½ cwt (2,422 lb).
Lb per c.c. (laden): 3.02.

BRAKES: Type: F, two-leading shoe; R, leading and trailing.
Method of operation: F, hydraulic; R, hydraulic.
Drum dimensions: F, 7in diameter; 1¼in wide. R, 7in diameter; 1¼in wide.
Lining area: F, 30¼ sq in. R, 30¼ sq in (56.4 sq in per ton laden).

TYRES: 5.90—13in.
Pressures (lb per sq in): F, 16; R, 23 (normal).

TANK CAPACITY: 5¾ Imperial gallons.
Oil sump, 6 pints.
Cooling system, 8½ pints.

TURNING CIRCLE: 35ft (L and R).
Steering wheel turns (lock to lock): 2¼.

DIMENSIONS: Wheelbase: 6ft 7½in.
Track: F, 3ft 9¼in; R, 3ft 8¾in.
Length (overall): 11ft 5¾in.
Height: 5ft 3in.
Width: 4ft 8in.
Ground clearance: 7in.
Frontal area: 18 sq ft (approximately).

ELECTRICAL SYSTEM: 12-volt; 32 ampère-hour battery.
Head lights: Double dip; 42-36 watt bulbs.

SUSPENSION: Front, independent, coil springs and wishbones. Rear, half-elliptic reverse camber leaf springs. Anti-roll bar position, rear.

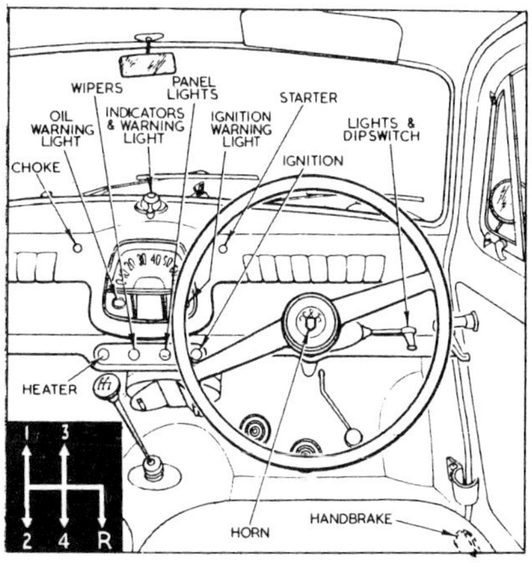
WIPERS
PANEL LIGHTS
STARTER
OIL WARNING LIGHT
INDICATORS & WARNING LIGHT
IGNITION WARNING LIGHT
LIGHTS & DIPSWITCH
CHOKE
IGNITION
HEATER
HORN
HANDBRAKE
1 3
2 4 R

The Motor Road Test No. 28/56

Make: Austin.   **Type:** A35 Seven 2-door de luxe saloon
Makers: The Austin Motor Co., Ltd., Longbridge, Birmingham

Test Data

CONDITIONS: Weather: Cool, dry, light breeze. (Temperature 45°—52°F., Barometer 30.3—30.4 in. Hg.) Surface: Dry tarmacadam. Fuel: Premium grade, approximately 95 Research Method Octane Rating.

INSTRUMENTS

Speedometer at 30 m.p.h.	7% fast
Speedometer at 60 m.p.h.	1% fast
Distance recorder	accurate

WEIGHT

Kerb weight (unladen, but with oil, coolant and fuel for approx. 50 miles)	14 cwt.
Front/rear distribution of kerb weight	57/43
Weight laden as tested	17½ cwt.

MAXIMUM SPEEDS

Flying Quarter Mile

Mean of four opposite runs	71.9 m.p.h.
Best one-way time equals	73.2 m.p.h.

"Maximile" Speed (Timed quarter mile after one mile accelerating from rest.)

Mean of four opposite runs	70.6 m.p.h.
Best one-way time equals	71.4 m.p.h.

Speed in Gears

Max. speed in 3rd gear	58 m.p.h.
Max. speed in 2nd gear	33 m.p.h.

FUEL CONSUMPTION

60.0 m.p.g. at constant 30 m.p.h. on level.
54.5 m.p.g. at constant 40 m.p.h. on level.
44.5 m.p.g. at constant 50 m.p.h. on level.
36.5 m.p.g. at constant 60 m.p.h. on level.

Overall Fuel Consumption for 999 miles, 26.5 gallons, equals 37.7 m.p.g. (7.5 litres/100 km.)

Touring Fuel Consumption (m.p.g. at steady speed midway between 30 m.p.h. and maximum, less 5% allowance for acceleration). 41.5 m.p.g.

Fuel Tank Capacity (maker's figure) 5¾ gallons.

BRAKES from 30 m.p.h.

0.97g retardation (equivalent to 31 ft. stopping distance) with 100 lb. pedal pressure
0.60g retardation (equivalent to 50 ft. stopping distance) with 75 lb. pedal pressure
0.35g retardation (equivalent to 86 ft. stopping distance) with 50 lb. pedal pressure
0.10g retardation (equivalent to 300 ft. stopping distance) with 25 lb. pedal pressure

ACCELERATION TIMES from standstill

0-30 m.p.h.	6.8 sec.
0-40 m.p.h.	11.6 sec.
0-50 m.p.h.	18.7 sec.
0-60 m.p.h.	30.1 sec.
Standing quarter mile	23.5 sec.

ACCELERATION TIMES On Upper Ratios

	Direct Top	Direct 3rd
10-30 m.p.h.	12.4 sec.	8.1 sec.
20-40 m.p.h.	12.3 sec.	8.5 sec.
30-50 m.p.h.	14.1 sec.	11.5 sec.
40-60 m.p.h.	18.7 sec.	—

STEERING

Turning circle between kerbs:

Left	32½ feet
Right	33 feet
Turns of steering wheel from lock to lock	2¼

HILL CLIMBING at sustained steady speeds

Max. gradient on direct top gear	1 in 12.1 (Tapley 185 lb./ton)
Max. gradient on 3rd gear	1 in 7.8 (Tapley 285 lb./ton)
Max. gradient on 2nd gear	1 in 4.9 (Tapley 445 lb./ton)

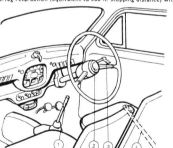

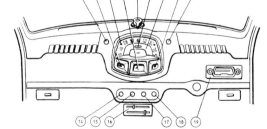

1, Gear lever. 2, Horn button. 3, Light switch and headlamp dip-switch. 4, Handbrake. 5, Choke control. 6, Oil pressure warning light. 7, Headlamp main beam indicator light. 8, Fuel contents gauge. 9, Direction indicator switch and repeater light. 10, Mileage recorder. 11, Speedometer. 12, Dynamo charge warning light. 13, Starter switch. 14, Heater fan switch. 15, Windscreen wiper switch. 16, Heater and demister control quadrants. 17, Panel light switch. 18, Ignition switch. 19 Radio controls.

The AUSTIN A35 De Luxe Two-door Saloon

ENLARGED and painted, but with a chrome surround, the radiator grille identifies the A35 front view from that of the lower-performance A30 from which it has been derived.

Larger Engine and New Gearbox Transform Performance of B.M.C. Economy Model

WHEN the Midland Editor of *The Motor* visited Longbridge shortly before the Motor Show to obtain details of the 1957 range, Austin engineers summed up their objectives for the new season as more power with greater economy. Although at first thought this may seem to run contrary to the old adage about not being able to have one's cake and eat it, there exist sound technical reasons for regarding it as by no means impossible. In consequence, the opportunity of taking over an A35 model for road test was seized with more than usual interest.

The model tried was the two-door de luxe saloon with, of course, the latest 948 c.c. engine which is a development of the former 803 c.c. type and, besides a larger capacity, has a full-flow oil filter and the more expensive lead-indium bearings which, as recent B.M.C. tests on German Autobahnen (when 25,000 miles were covered at 60 m.p.h.) conclusively proved, are much superior to the former type for sustained hard driving.

Comparison of the performance figures

obtained with this latest A35 with those recorded for the former A30 two-door saloon (vide *The Motor*, June 2, 1954) are significant.

Taking fuel consumption at constant speeds first, the A35 showed a gain of 2.6% at 30 m.p.h. with the very notable figure of 60 m.p.g. At 40 m.p.h. the improvement increased to 4.8%, whilst at 50 m.p.h. and 60 m.p.h. there was nothing to choose between the two, with the very minor gain of 1.3% at the former speed and an equally small loss of 1.4% at 60 m.p.h. Thus the balance is appreciably in favour of the new model for the sort of cruising speeds many drivers of this type of car adopt, with a small margin in hand for those who wish to take advantage of the improved acceleration of the new model without sacrifice of economy. Thus half of the Austin engineers' objective has obviously been fulfilled.

In connection with this aspect of performance, it is worth recording that the overall fuel consumption check was broken down into two sections, the first 380 miles

comprising some town running, about 100 miles cruising at a true 60 m.p.h. and the remainder at cruising speeds of 40-50 m.p.h.—a very typical cross-section of many owners' usage. This showed a consumption of 40.6 m.p.g. which, as a matter of interest, is remarkably close to the calculated "Touring Fuel Consumption" figure (41.5 m.p.g. in this case) which has been adopted as a new feature of *The Motor* road tests. The complete overall figure of 37.7 m.p.g. for 999 miles included performance tests and a large amount of hard driving.

So much for fuel consumptions. When it comes to speed and acceleration, the gains shown by the new model are very pronounced indeed. With a maximum mean speed of 71.9 m.p.h., the A35 is 11.1% faster than its predecessor, whilst acceleration figures from a standing start show improvements ranging from 20% in the times taken to reach 30 m.p.h. and 40 m.p.h. to a gain of nearly 29% in the 0-60 m.p.h. figure. As for acceleration in top gear, the smallest gain (from 20 m.p.h.

In Brief

Price: £368 17s. 6d. plus purchase tax £185 12s. 0d. equals £554 9s. 6d.
Capacity ... ... 948 c.c.
Unladen kerb weight ... 14 cwt.
Acceleration:
  10-30 m.p.h. in top gear ... 12.4 sec.
  0-50 m.p.h. through gears 18.7 sec.
Maximum direct top gear
  gradient ... ... 1 in 12.1
Maximum speed ... ... 71.9 m.p.h.
Maximile speed ... ... 70.6 m.p.h.
Touring fuel consumption ... 41.5 m.p.g.
Gearing: 14.26 m.p.h. in top gear at 1,000 r.p.m.; 28.5 m.p.h. at 1,000 ft./min. piston speed.

SPACE around the engine makes most mechanical components easy to reach, oil dipstick location being indicated here. Greater cylinder bore, a higher compression and strengthened crankshaft and bearings are new engine features.

INTERIOR feature of the latest small Austin is the sports-car type lever controlling a much improved gearbox. Individual front seats can be tipped forward to give access to a rear compartment adequate to give two adults reasonable comfort.

to 40 m.p.h.) was 18% and the largest, which, as might be expected, is in the 40-60 m.p.h. figure, is no less than 33.7%.

In short, in terms of pure figures, the higher compression and increased size of the new engine, coupled with the higher and more appropriate gearing, have very amply achieved their object.

Pure figures, however, are only half of the performance story of any car. What is just as important—and to many even more so—is how available performance can be used in terms of everyday driving. In this case, it is no overstatement to say that the new engine and gearbox have transformed this smallest Austin completely. In its outstanding handiness for business use in big cities or for the local day-to-day excursions of a family, it remains the likeable little car it always has been, but with an added liveliness that now makes it one of the quickest point-to-point means of transport in big towns that has ever been produced.

Out of Town

On the open road, the difference is even more marked because the improved acceleration and hill-climbing place it in an entirely different class, especially in the matter of easier overtaking. Greatly added facility in this respect, coupled with an ability to cruise at higher speeds without worry, make the new A35 a distinctly quick form of point-to-point transport on country roads as well as in towns.

As the German Autobahn tests mentioned earlier emphasize, a genuine 60 m.p.h. cruising speed is well within its capabilities. Above 50 m.p.h. engine vibration is rather evident by present-day standards, but in no way detracted from the willing feel of the engine or altered the fact that the A35 seemed to settle naturally to a mile-a-minute gait on a long run.

Although the high compression of the latest engine is noticeable in this way and

in a rougher tick-over, it has had no adverse effect on the flexibility of the unit at low speeds, 15 m.p.h. being a pace at which it will run happily and from which it will accelerate quite readily in top gear.

On the other hand, the new gearbox and, in particular, the new "sports car" gear lever, give every incentive to make full use of the gears. Indeed, the remote control of this model makes one realize what big sacrifices have been made in recent years in slavishly following the American practice of transferring the gearchange from its proper place to the end of a complicated system of rods or cables on the steering column. The new gear lever is nicely placed, has a moderate travel, and a positive action that is altogether delightful. It is possible to "beat" the synchromesh mechanism by hasty use, but the change is quick in any case.

Third gear provides a possible 58 m.p.h. and 50 m.p.h. is within its easy everyday scope, thus giving every encouragement to make full use of this ratio for acceleration and overtaking. Whilst by no means in-

audible, the indirect gears reach a very acceptable standard of quiet running, but the rear axle of the car tried was not as quiet as it might have been.

To revert to the power unit, no pinking occurred with premium fuel, the engine displayed no flat spots, started readily, and warmed up quickly. All the components requiring routine maintenance are, moreover, easily accessible through the top-opening bonnet aperture.

The handling qualities of the A35 may be classed as good, although the characteristics brought about by the short wheelbase, narrow track and a rear anti-roll bar strike a strange driver as somewhat unusual.

LUGGAGE accommodation in the rear locker is scaled by a 2-gallon petrol tin in the right-hand corner. Other details are the self-supporting locker lid, side-mounted spare wheel, and flashing direction indicators separate from the stop/tail lamps.

On corners, there is surprisingly little roll, but a definite feeling of weight transference from the inside to the outside rear wheel produces the impression of a pronounced oversteer which does not truly exist.

Once the driver becomes used to this, corners can be taken fast with confidence and if the speed should prove to be slightly exuberant, a quick twitch of the light and high-geared steering immediately puts matters right. The steering is free from unpleasant road reaction and has a quick and accurate response. In relation to the lightness of other controls, the brake

November 21, 1956   697   THE MOTOR

The AUSTIN A35 de Luxe Two-door Saloon

pedal needs surprisingly high pressure.

Despite the short wheelbase, pitching is absent and the general ride in both front and rear seats extremely comfortable, but a good deal of road noise comes into the car over certain surfaces.

In the main, the controls are very well arranged—especially the finger-tip light switch. Despite the fact that this A35 is one of the most compact cars on the market today, there is room for the wearer of a wide size 9 shoe to place his left foot beside the clutch, whilst, on the other hand, the accelerator and brakes are sufficiently near for "heel-and-toe" operation. Another good point is that the choke and starter controls are distinct from the minor switches, but the warning light of the non-cancelling direction-indicator switch is distinctly too bright for night-time use. The handbrake is neatly positioned to the outside of the driver's seat and is handy as well as powerful. Even better, however, would be a position between the seats adjacent to the new gear lever, so that one hand only would be needed for restarting on a gradient.

The new wide rear window is a very great improvement and, save for one point, the general vision is excellent, with a view of both front wings and a good upward angle of vision which is an advantage both when touring and when trying to read street names in towns. To the side, however, the view through the screen is somewhat limited by the main pillars.

In general passenger accommodation, the A35 remains a masterpiece of clever planning. It was originally designed to provide adequate, but not generous, seating for four persons within minimum overall dimensions, and that object it achieves supremely well. Thus, by suitable seat adjustment, four average-sized adults can be carried in comfort though not in luxury. Access to both front and rear (via tipping

VISION towards the rear of the A35 is enhanced by a new rear window of wrap-around curved shape. Four-door bodywork of similar outline is an option to the two-door style tested and illustrated.

front seats) entails no contortions and the seats are comfortable; in the front, in fact, they are much more so than their small dimensions might suggest and a 5 ft. 10½ in. driver found himself in no way cramped after a continuous two-and-a-half-hour spell at the wheel.

The driver's seat has a sliding adjustment and can readily be removed complete for picnicking, whilst the front passenger's seat has a three-position, spring-clip location which also allows of easy removal, but calls for the seat being tipped up before adjustment can be made.

In a small saloon, ventilation is particularly important and this problem has been well tackled in the de luxe model tested. Not only are there the usual hinged ventilating panels on the front doors (the main windows are of the drop pattern, without winders), but the rear quarter lights are hinged to provide an extractor effect. The heater, offered as an extra, is of the fresh-air type and provides an adequate warmth for normal winter conditions.

A minor criticism of the doors is that they are apt to swing-to annoyingly, but it must be remembered that this car is one of the cheapest on the market today and some refinements must, of necessity, be omitted. Indeed, the standard of finish and equipment on the A35 is surprisingly good, nothing that is essential being left out and the general finish and furnishings having nothing of the austerity touch about them.

Luggage accommodation is provided by a very useful rear boot, whilst a parcel shelf running right across the car below the facia board offers convenient space for odds and ends.

In short, the A35 represents an extremely good example of conventional design in minimum four-seater size at minimum cost. At unaltered price and with greatly improved performance, it should make more friends than ever.

Specification

Engine

Cylinders	4
Bore	62.9 mm.
Stroke	76.2 mm.
Cubic capacity	948 c.c.
Piston area	19.29 sq. in.
Valves	Overhead (pushrod)
Compression ratio	8.3/1
Carburetter	Zenith downdraught (26 VME)
Fuel pump	AC mechanical (Y type)
Ignition timing control	Centrifugal and vacuum
Oil filter	Full-flow
Max. power (net)	34 b.h.p.
at	4,750 r.p.m.
Piston speed at max. b.h.p.	2,375 ft./min.

Transmission

Clutch	Borg and Beck s.d.p.
Top gear (s/m)	4.55
3rd gear (s/m)	6.42
2nd gear (s/m)	10.79
1st gear	16.50
Reverse	21.22
Propeller shaft	Hardy Spicer open
Final drive	Hypoid bevel
Top gear m.p.h. at 1,000 r.p.m.	14.26
Top gear m.p.h. at 1,000 ft./min. piston speed	28.5

Chassis

Brakes	Lockheed hydraulic (2 l.s. on front)
Brake drum internal diameter	7 in.
Friction lining area	61 sq. in.
Suspension:	
Front	Independent (coil and wishbone)
Rear	Semi-elliptic with anti-roll bar
Shock absorbers	Lever-type hydraulic
Steering gear	Cam and peg
Tyres	5.20—13 tubeless

Coachwork and Equipment

Starting handle	Yes
Battery mounting	On scuttle
Jack	Smith's Steadylift
Jacking points	One (central) on each side
Standard tool kit: Jack, combined starting handle and wheelbrace, tyre pump, grease gun, screwdriver, tappet gauge, contact breaker and sparking plug gauge, tyre valve tool.	
Exterior lights: Two head, two side, two stop/tail, rear number plate lamp.	
Number of electrical fuses	Two
Direction indicators	Amber flasher type, non-self-cancelling
Windscreen wipers	Two-blade electrical, non self-parking
Windscreen washers	No
Sun vizors	One, hinge mounted
Instruments: Speedometer with non-decimal non-trip distance recorder, fuel contents gauge.	

Warning lights: Dynamo charge, oil pressure, headlamp main beam, direction-indicators.	
Locks:	
With ignition key	Ignition, driver's door and boot
With other key	Nil
Glove lockers	Nil
Map pockets	Nil
Parcel shelves	Below facia (full width)
Ashtrays	Two (below parcel shelf)
Cigar lighters	Nil
Interior lights: One below instrument panel operated by courtesy switches on doors.	
Interior heater	Extra
Car radio	Extra
Extras available	Passenger's sun vizor, radio, heater-demister
Upholstery material	PVC-coated fabric
Floor covering	Carpets
Number of exterior colours standardized	Eight
Alternative body styles	Four-door saloon

Maintenance

Sump	7 pints (incl. filter) S.A.E. 30 (summer), (20 winter)
Gearbox	2¼ pints, S.A.E. 40
Rear axle	1¼ pints, S.A.E. 90 hypoid
Steering gear lubricant	S.A.E. 140 gear oil
Cooling system capacity	8¼ pints (2 drain taps)
Chassis lubrication	By grease gun every 1,000 miles to 15 points
Ignition timing	5 degrees B.T.D.C.
Spark plug type	Champion NA8, 14 mm.
Spark plug gap	0.025 in.
Contact breaker gap	0.014-0.016 in.
Valve timing: Inlet opens 5 degrees B.T.D.C. and closes 45 degrees A.B.D.C. Exhaust opens	

40 degrees B.B.D.C. and closes 10 degrees A.T.D.C.	
Tappet clearances (hot or cold):	
Inlet	0.012 in.
Exhaust	0.012 in.
Front wheel toe-in	1/16 in.
Camber angle	1 degree
Castor angle	3 degrees
Steering swivel pin inclination	6¼ degrees
Tyre pressures:	
Front	20 lb.
Rear	20-23 lb. according to load
Brake fluid	Lockheed
Battery type and capacity	Lucas 12- volt, 38 amp./hr.

THE AUTOCAR,
4 JULY 1958

Amber winking indicator lamps are placed below the head lamps: side lamps are mounted on the front wings where they can be seen by the driver. Bumper - overriders are standard on the de luxe model

Autocar ROAD TESTS 1690

Austin A.35
FOUR-DOOR DE LUXE

WELL-RECEIVED when it first appeared at Earls Court in 1952, the small Austin has enjoyed increasing popularity, particularly since the introduction of the 948 c.c. engine in 1956. More recently there has been wider appreciation of the car's performance and handling, and nowadays it is commonplace at race meetings for modified Austin A.35s to compete with a high degree of success in production car events. This test of a four-door model (the two-door A.35 was road tested on 28 December, 1956) provided a welcome opportunity to recall the qualities of this popular little car.

In the four-door saloon the front doors are 9in narrower than those of the two-door version, but access to both front and rear compartments is still easy. The doors open almost to a 90 deg angle, but there are no retaining catches to hold them open. As on the two-door model, the individual front seats can be tilted forward, but the backrest and squab are not hinged separately. The rear door windows are fixed, but there are swivelling rear quarter lights which can be used to good effect in warm weather to circulate a stream of fresh air within the car. For the two extra doors the total price of the de luxe model, including purchase tax, is increased by £18 (£26 on the standard models), but in addition to the convenience for those who frequently carry a full complement of passengers, the appearance of the four-door version is generally thought to be better.

Convenient direct-lift windows are fitted in the front doors, and to raise or lower there are small glass rectangular finger grips on the inner surfaces. When the interior door handles are raised to the locked position the windows are secured against movement from outside if they are fully up or open half an inch. The driver's door can be locked only by key.

Rearward visibility through the wide wrap-round window is excellent; but the small width of the flat windscreen results in the screen pillars being somewhat obstructive of the otherwise good forward vision. To drivers of average height the raised side lamps are clearly visible.

The seats, particularly in the front, are very comfortable, and long journeys in the A.35 do not involve cramp or thigh discomfort, but the otherwise good driving position is marred by the awkward positioning of the pedals. The brake and accelerator pedals are both too near the floor; unfortunately, because of the intrusion of the front wheel arch it is difficult to see how this could be avoided, but possibly a reduction of about two inches in the length of the throttle pedal shank would effect an improvement.

In the central instrument nacelle is mounted the speedometer; it is clear and easy to read but has no trip mileage recorder. Below it is the fuel gauge, with warning lamps for oil pressure (on its left) and ignition (right).

The ignition keyhole, separate pull-out starter control, switches for the optionally extra heater, the panel lamps, and windscreen wipers are all mounted centrally on the edge of the full-width parcels shelf. When either of the front doors is opened, these switches are illuminated by a low-power lamp bulb under the instrument cluster. The windscreen wipers clear a large area of the screen but are not self-parking.

In the warm weather which prevailed during the test there was no real opportunity to prove the efficiency of the heater, other than to observe that the interior of the car became uncomfortably hot at the maximum setting when the heater was tried one morning after a cold start. It was possible to note, however, that the delivery of air for ventilation purposes at the cold setting was vigorous and well balanced throughout the interior, with a noticeably quiet-running fan.

When the A.35 superseded the A.30, separate amber winking indicators were fitted fore and aft; and the signal which they give is unmistakeable. However, although it is now nearly two years since this change was made, the doors are still shaped to allow for the old semaphore indicators, and the indicator housings in the body are covered by metal plates held in place by screws. The control for the indicators is still a non-self-cancelling central switch at the top of

Under-bonnet space is full but not crowded. The coil is mounted on the dynamo, but the distributor protrudes from the engine low down where it is not easily accessible. The dip stick is too short for convenience

The doors open wide, and access to front or rear is easy. The upholstery is in p.v.c.-coated fabric, which appears to be durable: fluffy cloth is used for the roof linings. The front compartment floor is covered in moulded rubber, and there are carpets in the back. Neat chromium-plated handles replace the door-straps of the previous models

Austin A.35 4-door . . .

the facia, and it is inconvenient to use. A simple steering column-mounted lever would be better, and more in keeping with the excellent lights switch which protrudes on the right, and can be operated without removing a hand from the wheel. This switch rotates to provide three settings: side and tail lamps, dipped head lamps, and main beam. The single Windtone horn has a deep, penetrating note, and is sounded by the usual steering wheel button.

Five position fore-and-aft adjustment of the driving seat is provided; for the passenger seat there is a choice of three notches. In the fully back position a tall driver has room to stretch, and yet space for rear passengers is still reasonable if they are prepared to sit with one knee at each side of the seat in front of them. They are more critically conscious of the lack of tilt of the rear seat cushion, which tends to slide them off the seat. Also road noises are more noticeable in the rear seat than in the front; nevertheless the standard of comfort for passengers in such a small car is very creditable.

The driving position is splendid, with the lever for the effective handbrake conveniently to the right of the driving seat, and the short, remote-control gear lever centrally placed and well back, where it is easily reached.

This rigid and positive gear change, which would be a credit to any sports car, is a major factor in the pleasure of driving the A.35. Weaknesses of the gear box which detracted from this a little were that bottom gear was often difficult to engage from rest, and that the synchromesh was easily beaten if the lever was pulled through quickly, but changes are still speedy even if slower movements are used to compensate for this slight deficiency. With some care the car can be started in second, but bottom gear is there to be used, and the A.35 responds best to free use of all four ratios. In particular, third gear gives a lively performance in the important speed range from 30 to 50 m.p.h., and allows a maximum of 58 m.p.h.

No loss of smoothness results from the quite high compression ratio of 8.3 to 1, and the car would pick up speed

without complaint from 15 m.p.h. in top gear—equivalent to just a shade over 1,000 r.p.m. The engine starts readily hot or cold, and although even in warm weather the choke is needed for the first start of the day, it can be pushed home almost as soon as the engine fires. Once started, the power unit pulls without hesitation or stalling while warming-up.

It is often noticed how one characteristic is maintained in a particular model throughout the years. The A.35 can be regarded as a successor to the pre-war Austin Seven, and many will remember this famous vehicle for the rather abrupt action of the clutch. In some ways, unfortunately, the A.35 maintains this tradition. Operating load was light, but engagement occurred very suddenly during the last inch or so of pedal release, and unless the foot was brought back gently an abrupt take-up would result.

In the previous Austin A.35 Road Test, comment was made on the noisiness of the transmission, and this was again noticed in the latest car tried. Except on the over-run, a pronounced back axle whine was heard at about 50 m.p.h. in top gear, becoming more evident as 60 m.p.h. was approached. It is particularly unfortunate that this is the speed range that many owners would adopt for normal main road cruising. It is this alone that reminds the driver that engine revs have passed the 4,000 r.p.m. mark; 60-65 m.p.h. may still be held without feeling that the engine is being overworked. On the test there were no loss of tune or signs of stress when 70 m.p.h. was held for long periods.

Driven thus, the car remains stable, and a light hold on the steering wheel is sufficient to maintain a straight course without wander. An even higher opinion of the car's road-holding may be formed when it has been taken through sharp, ill-cambered corners at speed. There is little tyre squeal, and the mild oversteering tendency gives confidence to the driver when the car is near the point of breakaway, particularly as the car responds quickly to corrective action. With tyre pressures about 3lb sq in above the maker's recommendation for the fully laden condition of 20 front, 23 rear, cornering was improved still further, but there was then less warning when the limit of adhesion was approached, particularly on wet roads.

From the feel of the steering it may be thought at first that the ratio is too low, because the effort required at the wheel is small, even when manœuvring; but the gearing is just right at 2¼ turns from lock to lock, and there is no noticeable lost movement.

The suspension is a good compromise between the needs of comfort and stability, in a car which must accommodate a wide variation of passenger load in relation to its unladen weight. With the driver only aboard, the car is rather firm, and on very rough roads there are some quick vertical pitching movements. Fully laden, the ride is excellent; potholes and smaller road irregularities are ironed out without transmitting much noise to the inside of the car. Even so this is not a vehicle to drive fast over bad roads.

Although the brakes were reassuringly effective in normal use, it was found during the test that surprisingly high pedal pressures were necessary to achieve rapid retardation.

One of the most impressive features about the car—partly related, no doubt, to its high compression—is the ability to return petrol consumption figures consistently above 40 m.p.g., even when driven hard. The figure of 41.8 m.p.g.

External hinges alone interrupt the lines of the car; many consider that the four-door A.35 looks more attractive than the two-door

Austin A.35 4-door . . .

recorded in the data table includes many miles in London traffic and a number of journeys in which, as already mentioned, the car was driven to the limit.

On another journey on which the car was driven more gently and the speedometer was maintained between 50 and 60 m.p.h. whenever practicable 44 and 47 miles were recorded on successive gallons. Most owners would have no difficulty in obtaining 100 miles from ten shillings worth of premium fuel.

The model tested was the de luxe version of the four-door saloon. It is distinguished by drawer-type ashtrays in the front compartment and bumper over-riders.

Most owners will be disappointed when they open the tool-kit. A blunt-edged, "bent-wire" type of screwdriver, a box spanner, a tyre valve and key, jack and hand pump are all that is provided. It would be an improvement if the last item, which few owners use at all these days, were replaced by some spanners. Home maintenance is often important to the owner of such a vehicle; there are 19 greasing points, in addition to several items on the throttle and pedal linkage which need oiling every 1,000 miles.

Even bearing in mind the economy of the A.35, the 5¾-gallon petrol tank is still on the small side, and results in frequent stops to buy comparatively small quantities of petrol. But this and the few other points mentioned are minor shortcomings which detract little from the first-class overall impression which the car creates.

In addition to its excellent fuel economy, it is specially remembered for the way in which, in dense traffic conditions, its nippy performance and compact dimensions made it a fast car from point to point, and one which could usually be parked without difficulty on arrival.

AUSTIN A.35 4-DOOR DE LUXE

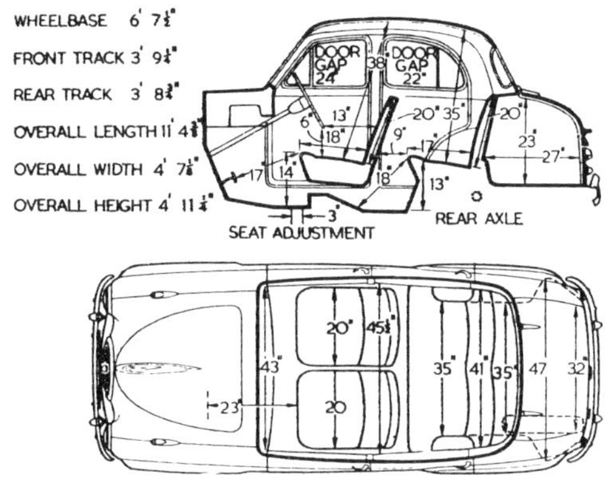
WHEELBASE 6' 7½"
FRONT TRACK 3' 9¼"
REAR TRACK 3' 8¾"
OVERALL LENGTH 11' 4⅝"
OVERALL WIDTH 4' 7⅛"
OVERALL HEIGHT 4' 11¼"
DOOR GAP 24"
DOOR GAP 22"
SEAT ADJUSTMENT
REAR AXLE

Scale ¼in to 1ft. Driving seat in central position. Cushion uncompressed.

DATA

PRICE (basic), with de luxe four-door body, **£400.**
British purchase tax, **£201 7s.**
Total (in Great Britain), **£601 7s.**
Extras: Radio **£25.** Heater **£20 16s 3d.**

ENGINE: Capacity: 948 c.c. (57.8 cu in).
Number of cylinders: 4.
Bore and stroke: 62.9 × 76.2 mm (2.5 × 3.0in).
Valve gear: o.h.v., pushrods.
Compression ratio: 8.3 to 1.
B.H.P.: 34 (nett) at 4,750 r.p.m. (B.H.P. per ton laden 39.8).
Torque: 50 lb ft at 2,000 r.p.m.
M.P.H. per 1,000 r.p.m. on top gear, 14.3.

WEIGHT: (with 5 gals fuel), 14 cwt (1,575 lb).
Weight distribution (per cent): F, 58; R, 42.
Laden as tested: 17 cwt (1,911 lb).
Lb per c.c. (laden): 2.02

BRAKES: Type: Lockheed.
Method of operation: hydraulic.
Drum dimensions: F, 7in diameter; 1¼in wide. R, 7in diameter; 1¼in wide.
Lining area: F, 30.5 sq in. R, 30.5 sq in. (82 sq in per ton laden).

TYRES: 5.20—13in.
Pressures (lb per sq in): F, 20; R, 20-23 (according to load).

TANK CAPACITY: 5¾ Imperial gallons.
Oil sump, 6 pints.
Cooling system, 8½ pints.

STEERING: turning circle:
Between kerbs 33ft 1in.
Between walls 34ft 4in.
Turns of steering wheel from lock to lock 2⅓.

DIMENSIONS: Wheelbase: 6ft 7½in.
Track: F, 3ft 9¼in; R, 3ft 8¾in.
Length (overall): 11ft 4⅝in.
Height: 4ft 11¼in.
Width: 4ft 7⅛in.
Ground clearance: 6⅜in.
Frontal area: 16.9 sq ft (approximately).

ELECTRICAL SYSTEM: 12-volt; 38 ampere-hour battery.
Head lights: Double dip; 42—36 watt bulbs.

SUSPENSION: Front, Independent, coil springs and wishbones. Rear, Semi-elliptic springs with live axle and anti-roll bar.

PERFORMANCE

ACCELERATION: from constant speeds.
Speed Range, Gear ratios and Time in sec.

M.P.H.	4.55 to 1	6.42 to 1	10.8 to 1	16.51 to 1
10—30..	—	8.7	5.7	—
20—40..	12.6	8.5	—	—
30—50..	13.1	10.8	—	—
40—60..	17.9	—	—	—

From rest through gears to:

M.P.H.	sec.
30	7.1
40	11.9
50	19.1
60	31.0

Standing quarter mile, 23.7 sec.

MAXIMUM SPEEDS ON GEARS:

Gear		M.P.H.	K.P.H.
Top ..	**(mean)**	**72.8**	**117.1**
	(best)	**75**	**120.7**
3rd ..	.. ..	**58**	**93.3**
2nd ..	.. ..	**34**	**54.7**
1st ..	.. ..	**22**	**35.4**

TRACTIVE EFFORT:

	Pull (lb per ton)	Equivalent Gradient
Top	174	12.7
Third	259	8.6
Second..	360	6.1

BRAKES (at 30 m.p.h. in neutral):

Pedal load in lb	Retardation	Equivalent stopping distance in ft
50	0.32g	94
75	0.60g	49
100	0.84g	36

FUEL CONSUMPTION:

M.P.G. at steady speeds

M.P.H.	Top
30	59.8
40	54.0
50	46.5
60	37.7
70	32.2

41.8 m.p.g. overall for 1,925 miles (6.8 litres per 100 km).

Approximate normal range 40–48 m.p.g. (7.1–5.9 litres per 100 km).

TEST CONDITIONS: Weather: dry, sunny, no wind, air temperature 65 deg. F.

Road surface, dry tarmacadam. Fuel, premium grade.

Acceleration figures are the means of several runs in opposite directions.

Tractive effort obtained by Tapley meter.

SPEEDOMETER CORRECTION: M.P.H.

Car speedometer:	10	20	30	40	50	60	70	75
True speed:	8	18	27	37	47	57	67	71

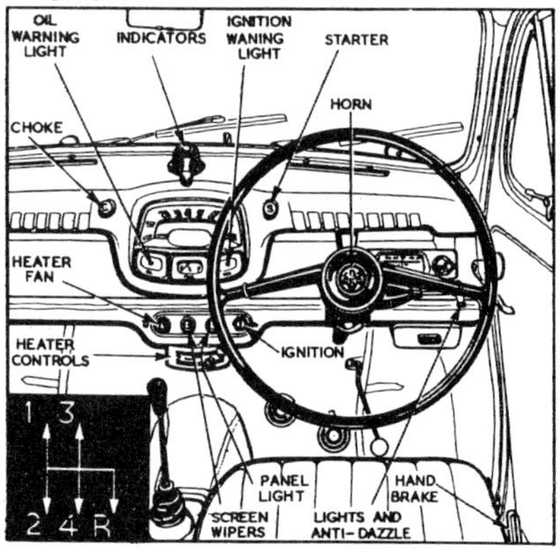
OIL WARNING LIGHT
INDICATORS
IGNITION WANING LIGHT
STARTER
HORN
CHOKE
HEATER FAN
HEATER CONTROLS
IGNITION
1 3
2 4 R
PANEL LIGHT
HAND BRAKE
SCREEN WIPERS
LIGHTS AND ANTI-DAZZLE

OWNER'S VIEW

Kim Henson interviews David Lovering, of Bournemouth, Dorset, who owns a 1955 A30 two door saloon. His hobby is restoring and using old vehicles, and he also owns a 1934 Ford Model 'Y' and a 1946 Standard Flying Eight.

K.H. Why are you so interested in the A30?
D.L. It is a neat, practical car and ideal for everyday use. I own two older cars and a modern Opel, and the A30 fits in very nicely – it is interesting yet entirely usable in today's traffic.
K.H. When did you buy your A30, and why?
D.L. I bought the car in 1978 from a friend. He had rescued it from dereliction on a Dorset farm and his temporary accommodation for the car had to be vacated, so I told him that he could park it on my patio ... there it remained for several months with the original intention that it would be broken up and used for spares for his A30. However, as time passed, we talked ourselves into renovating it!
K.H. So what sort of condition was it in?
D.L. Absolutely shocking! It had been sitting in a muddy field for four years prior to my acquisition of it, and, as it had no wheels at the time, a lot of the underbody had

suffered terribly. The wings at the front were almost non-existent, the rear spring-hangers likewise, and the brakes were seized solid.

The luggage boot had been used for carrying liquid concrete by the farmer – apparently he had bought the car for ferrying this to the site of a new outbuilding! The stuff had set solid in all the corners. The interior was full of tractor parts and squirrels were in residence under the bonnet ...

To sum up our problems, we took it on a trailer to two professional welders who both said that the car was 'too far gone' for restoration.
K.H. So how did you tackle the job?
D.L. A little at a time. Stripping the car bit by bit, we made up new sections for the bodywork by hand, at home, including new inner wing panels. We engaged a brave welder who set to work for us and gradually rebuilt the underbody. I bought two good secondhand wings from a breaker's, fitted them, and then we resprayed the car top to bottom, inside and out.

My wife tackled the upholstery, and at length the car looked ready.
K.H. What about the mechanical jobs?
D.L. That's where we struck very lucky. It soon became evident that the engine and gearbox were both BMC 'Gold Seal' replacements, and they both worked well, despite their years in the open. In fact the only restoration work needed was to clean the carburettor!

The brakes, of course, needed total renewal, including all the pipework, but the steering was in good shape.
K.H. Would it have been a better bet to buy a car in tidier condition?
D.L. Logically, yes, but there's more to it than that ... the task became a challenge and, when we finished the car, all the work proved to be worthwhile.
K.H. What about spare parts?
D.L. We obtained most of the bodywork bits we needed from breakers' yards, but all the

mechanical items were available from local parts factors and Austin dealers.
K.H. Is your car used everyday?
D.L. Yes, it is, all year round, rain or shine – it has to earn its keep. In fact my wife sold her Cortina when she saw the finished A30 restoration, and she now uses the little Austin daily.
K.H. What kind of performance and handling does the A30 have?
D.L. With only 800ccs to play with obviously it's not a sports car, but it does go very well, and will cruise all day at 50–55mph. The A30's low third gear is excellent for town use – you can pull away quite happily from walking pace. Handling? I've always found it very good, but then the car isn't used for performance driving.
K.H. Do you enter the car for concours events – presumably you don't use it for motorsport?
D.L. Motorsport, no – I think that's probably more suited to hotted up A35s. As to concours, no, although we often take the A30 out for local old car runs and to some of the 'static' rallies. We prefer to actually use the car.
K.H. Are you a member of the Owners' Club?
D.L. Not yet, although it's something I should like to do in the future.
K.H. Is there a specialist whom you have found particularly useful?
D.L. Well, I get most of the routine maintenance items from local parts factors and specialist knowledge from my friends who know the cars well!
K.H. How would you sum up the enjoyment you get from your A30?
D.L. It's a cute, 'friendly' little vehicle, with a lot of appeal. Having said that, my wife needs a car to be 100 per cent reliable in all weathers, with, occasionally, four seats and room for all the shopping too.

The A30 (we call her 'Judy' because of her number, 'JDY 4') has all these assets. On top of that she is cheap to run and to maintain, and she has more

31

character than most cars. A delight to own.

K.H. Finally, what advice would you give to potential owners?

D.L. What are you waiting for? Get in there and buy one!

Kim Henson interviews Paul Card, of Croydon in Surrey, who owns an immaculate show-winning 1957 two door A35. Paul is car mad (according to his wife at least!), and spends most of his free time keeping his pristine Austin in that condition.

K.H. When did you first become interested in the A35?

P.C. Well, I bought this car four years ago with the intention of bringing it back as near as possible to 'original' condition.

K.H. What sort of work did you have to do to the car?

P.C. When I bought this Austin, it wasn't in too bad a state, bodily at least. However, the brakes had decayed over the years, and the windscreen seal was so perished that the screen was actually falling out! The main restoration work consisted of removing the main mechanical units (for respraying the engine bay), and overhauling the brakes. While the engine was out, I also renewed the clutch and engine mountings. The body, too, was resprayed, in the original 'Court Grey'.

K.H. Is the car otherwise original?

P.C. Yes – the engine has covered 46,000 miles, as has the gearbox, from new. The car even has the original rubber interior mat.

K.H. Did you experience any difficulty in obtaining the parts you needed for the restoration?

P.C. No, not really. Most of the mechanical spares are still to be found, although I realise that body parts are difficult to obtain.

K.H. Are the problems you had to overcome on your car fairly typical?

P.C. Yes – brakes on these cars are often neglected, for example. I

think, though, that I was perhaps lucky to get such a solid car to start with – that alone saved a lot of time and money.

K.H. Do you use the car every day?

P.C. No, it is used more as an enjoyable means of weekend transport, although it is very practical and cheap to run.

K.H. How would you rate the performance and handling of the A35?

P.C. The performance is very good, especially considering its age and engine size. The handling, though, is not surprisingly a little less 'taut' than on modern cars.

K.H. Has your car won many prizes and concours awards?

P.C. Yes, it has taken quite a few awards, particularly in rallies organised by the A30/A35 Owners' Club. For example, it was overall winner at the 1983 National Rally, second in the 'Supreme' class at the 1984 National Rally, first in the A35 class at the 1982 Southern Counties Rally, then first in the 'Supreme' class at the 1983, and first in the A35 class in the 1984 events.

K.H. Presumably, then, you don't enter the Austin in any form of motorsport?

P.C. No, I leave that to the enthusiasts, although I know that the A35 is a very competitive vehicle in Classic Saloon Car racing, for example.

K.H. You mentioned the A30/A35 Owners' Club – do they have many major events, and is it helpful to be a member?

P.C. Yes, they hold regular events on a national and regional basis, and even organize trips abroad. I find it a friendly club, and it's always helpful to be able to contact other people with an interest in the same type of vehicle.

K.H. Are there any particular specialists for obtaining parts for these cars?

P.C. Yes, it's possible to buy all sorts of spares from specialists, including, now, body repair panels and some of the rubber trim, etc. Many (particularly mechanical) parts can still be obtained from Austin Rover dealers, though.

K.H. How would you sum up the enjoyment you get from your A35, and what would you say to potential owners, thinking of buying one?

P.C. Truly a great little car. Parts are easy to obtain, when you need them, which isn't very often, but it's still nice to know, especially if a car is to be used daily. An A35 is strong, very reliable, easy to maintain and economical to run. With four seats and a big boot, what more could you ask?

BUYING

Models available

Nowadays there are very few of the original (AS3) A30s in general use. However the four door (AS4) and two door (A2S4) saloons are still to be found in comparatively large numbers, although the van (AV4) and Countryman (AP4) versions are to be regarded as rare vehicles today.

A35s are naturally rather more plentiful. The two door saloons (A2S5) outnumber the four door model (AS5) and, as with the A30, van and Countryman versions of the 948cc A35 (AV5 and AP5 respectively) are now rather scarce. Pick-ups were not built in great numbers originally, and so this model (AK5) is now, sadly, a very infrequent sight, with just a handful surviving.

The later vans are more commonly seen, particularly the AV8 models from the 'sixties, but the Mark II vans (AV6) and Countryman (AP6) are, again, a rare find today.

Which one?

The early A30s are very interesting from an historical point of view, in

particular the original model with the internal, cantilever boot hinges. Alas these are almost extinct as a breed now. Later AS3s are still around, though.

If you are considering one of these for everyday use, the only drawback could be the difficulty of supply of some spare parts unique to this model – doors, trim, speedometer, low ratio differentials, seats, and so on. Having said that, some spares (for example new chrome grilles) are more plentiful than for the later cars, since fewer of the AS3s survive and hence demand is less.

Apart from the slightly higher final drive ratio, driving one of the later A30s is similar to driving an early one. With the later cars you have the choice of two or four doors, which may be an important factor if you have young children.

The 803cc power unit used in all A30s is a tough, reliable engine which will give good economy unless the carburettor and distributor are well worn. However, it will not put up with consistently high revs for very long without complaint. After 50,000 miles or so of hard use (or less if you're very brutal) you will detect a light 'tapping' from the engine under light load conditions. This is often, at first, put down to 'tappet rattle' or 'little end tap' or even 'piston slap'. However, in nine cases out of ten, it is big end knock, which requires immediate attention if you want to avoid the need for a new crankshaft. These are both scarce and relatively expensive for the 803cc engine, unfortunately, and are unique to this motor.

Therefore, if you need a car for constant high speed use, an A35 would be a better bet (more about this later), or the 948cc engine can be fitted directly into the A30 (mating directly with the A30 gearbox) and looks very little different from the earlier unit.

The A30 gearbox can wear rapidly if used unsympathetically. First signs of trouble are weak synchromesh, slipping out of 2nd

and/or third gears on overrun, and uncertain selection of third gear, which can be fun in heavy traffic!

With a design which dates back to the pre-war Austin Eight, the ratios in the A30 gearbox are typically 'Austin', and rather low. The result is a fair step up between third and top gears. On the other hand, third gear is an ideal one for negotiating slow traffic (in towns, for example), or for climbing fairly steep hills. If you're at all kind to the car, though, anything much above 35mph in third gear is definitely too fast.

On all models, the rear axle and propeller shaft are pretty viceless and run for years without attention (apart from lubrication). However the clutch can sometimes be very fierce – if this proves to be so, renewal will cure the trouble. Depending on use, the new clutch components should then last at least 60,000 miles without further attention.

The A35 is very similar in character to the A30, but is mechanically much stronger. The 948cc engine, with its lead-indium lined bearings and full-flow oil filtration system, is far more suited to hard driving and high cruising speeds than its 803cc predecessor. In addition, the extra power of the A35 is very useful, especially when hill-climbing, towing, or overtaking fast traffic.

The gearbox was stronger too, with a slicker, remote control gearchange and higher intermediate ratios. While third gear on the A35 is not as good as the A30 for town work or steep hills, it is better from the point of view of high speed overtaking. Many prefer the A35 gearbox, but it's all a matter of personal preference and the use to which you put the car.

Problems with the A35 gearbox are few, but high mileage usually shows itself by way of noisy first and reverse gears, and weak synchromesh between the top three gears.

The 848cc and 1098cc

engines are also reliable units, the 848cc vans giving much the same performance as the 948cc cars, albeit with a slightly lower axle ratio, and the 1100 vans being particularly good for fast cruising.

Routine servicing items are readily available for the A35s, but with the A30, items such as the canister-type bypass oil filter, and the contact points, are getting a little scarce.

Engine parts on the 1100cc cars are common with those on the later Morris 1000 and Austin A40 Mark II, while the 848cc engine is basically the Mini unit, and the 948cc engine and the 803cc unit were also used in the first Morris 1000 and Morris Minor respectively.

The post-1956 engines are normally good for 100,000 miles plus without major overhaul, if regularly serviced.

Running gear

The front suspension and steering last well if regularly greased, but the lever arm shock absorbers are usually well worn after 20,000 miles or so, and in extreme cases cause severe fluttering and reverberations from the front wheels at speed and on hitting the slightest bump. If the front shockers are 'shot' the car will also corner like a blancmange! Renewal is straightforward and reconditioned units are easily available.

The king pins and bushes need regular attention from a greasegun, and the threaded fulcrum pin is used as a bearing. This design leads to fairly rapid wear if lubrication is neglected, and 'clonks' from the front over rough surfaces.

The rear suspension lasts very well, although the rear spring shackle bushes in the 'chassis' tubes wear after very high mileages.

For carrying heavy loads often, the stronger van springs can be fitted at the rear.

Bodywork

All A30s and A35s are now over their first flush of youth, and rust is an enemy, as with all cars. Places to investigate are the inner and outer sills, rear spring hanger areas, the base of each front wing, the front inner wings and the whole of the front panelwork of the car.

Road mud collects between the outer front panel and the inner radiator mounting area, and rust eats its way out from here if not checked regularly. The door bottoms also rust if neglected, as does the floor immediately behind the front wheels. Most such areas are fairly easily repairable by welding, however.

The interiors of all cars are very durable, but the door panels can warp if the rain deflectors in the doors have been disturbed.

Historical value patterns

The A30/35 range passed through its lowest price era during the late 'sixties and early 'seventies. Having said that, good roadworthy examples can still be purchased very reasonably, and prices have not escalated to the same degree as, for example, the Morris Minor. In fact, since the late 'seventies prices have remained comparatively steady, in real terms.

This is a good thing as far as most enthusiasts are concerned, since these cars are still affordable classics.

Summing up

An A30 or A35 is an ideal car for everyday use or pleasure only. If you do a lot of travelling, the A35 is a better bet – it has more power with no loss of economy, and engine and gearbox components are more readily available.

The A30 is now scarcer, and to many, a more interesting car, but still practical transport for a family.

If major rebuilds appeal, these cars are again ideal. There is plenty of room to get to most of the mechanical components for working on them and, rusty nuts excluded, most jobs are very straightforward.

The vans – many have been converted to estate cars – are practical load carriers and with a rear seat conversion make a very useful 'utility' vehicle. Many people of course prefer saloon cars, and there are still plenty to choose from, with an estimated 20,000 still on the road.

If you are thinking of buying an A30/35, look in the local newspaper's classified ads section, in *The Exchange and Mart* 'Collectors Cars' section, or in one of the specialist older car magazines. Many are also advertised in the A30/A35 Owners Club newsletters and magazines. You will soon find a car in the condition you require, at a price you can afford.

CLUBS, SPECIALISTS & BOOKS

Club

The **Austin A30/A35 Owners' Club** is an active organisation with approximately 1000 members.

It was started in the early 'seventies by keen enthusiast Steve Gilks, who still uses an A30 (albeit much modified!) regularly today. Steve set up the club with a constitution which aimed 'to maintain as many A30/35s in good working order as is possible, by helping, encouraging, advising and cultivating a spirit of friendship amongst members'.

Over the years the Club has grown in numbers, but its aims have remained the same. With members all over Britain and around the world, the Club's excellent quarterly magazine, *Spotlight* and regular newsletters in between, keep the enthusiasts in touch with the spares scene, national and regional Club events, trips abroad and technical topics, plus all sorts of facts and figures.

The Rallies are a major attraction in the Club calendar, and seeing other members' restored cars gives encouragement to those struggling with a long rebuild.

Sadly, the Club found it necessary to discontinue their own, comprehensive spares service, although they still have a spares co-ordinator, and some area groups run their own spares arrangements.

Specialists

There are many firms who can supply parts for the A30/35. Of particular interest are:

Autofurbish, 15, Ricroft Road, Compstall, Stockport, Cheshire, SK6 5JR, England. Tel: (061) 427 5292 – various spares.

The Austin A30 and A35 Centre, 'The Gables', 16, Hale Road, Heckington, Sleaford, Lincolnshire, NG34 9JW, England. Tel: (0529) 61049 – body repair panels, etc.

Bedworth Car Valet Service Ltd., George Street, Bedworth, Nr. Nuneaton, Warwickshire, CV12 8EB, England. Tel: (0203) 312291 – spares and rebuilds.

Eric Bentley, 1, Alms Hill Glade, Parkhead, Sheffield, Yorkshire, England – repro body panels, etc.

William Cochran, 25, Fiveheads Road, Horndean, Portsmouth, Hampshire, England – soft trim and rubber seals.

Steve Gilks, 17, Forest Close, Pinders Heath, Wakefield, West Yorkshire, England – servicing parts, etc.

Bob Mitchell, 18, Bridle Close, Chapleton, Sheffield, Yorkshire, England. Tel: (0724) 848837 – chromework.

Books

Comparatively little has been written about the A30/35 in recent years, but contemporary volumes such as the manufacturers' handbooks, workshop manuals and advertising leaflets can be obtained fairly readily from autojumbles, etc.

Other useful books, some of which were first published many years ago, are still very relevant today. They include:

The Cassell Book of the Austin A30 'Seven', 1951-56 by Ellison Hawkes. A pocket-sized book with a multitude of technical and overhaul information.

The Book of the Austin A30 and A35 by Staton Abbey, M.I.M.I., published by Pitman. A practical guide to maintenance and overhaul.

The Handbook for the Austin A30 and A35 by Piet Olyslager, M.S.I.A., M.S.A.E., published by the Sunday Times. A useful and interesting book full of general and technical information.

Haynes Owner's Handbook for the Austin A35 and A40 by B.L. Chalmers-Hunt. Packed with useful technical information.

Haynes Owners Workshop Manual for the Austin A35 and A40 by J.H. Haynes. A comprehensive guide to practical d.i.y. repair and maintenance of the Austin A30 and A35. Still in print.

A recent publication of interest to those who like facts and figures is the **Brooklands Books** collection of Road Tests and contemporary articles about the A30 and A35, compiled by R.M. Clarke.

PHOTO
GALLERY

1

1. Profile of an A30 – in this case a two door (A2S4) version. As with other Austins of the early 'fifties, the body lines are rounded and flowing; all the panels merging with one another.

2. With the sidelights prominently mounted on the wing tops, the front of the car has a straightforward, uncluttered look. The chrome grille panel of the A30 gives the car a smart frontal appearance, and adds to its character.

2

3

4

5

6

7

8

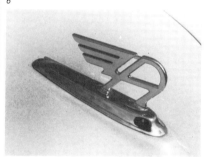
9

10

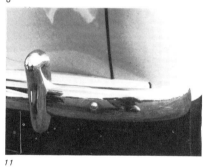
11

12

3. One of the most obvious external differences between the A30 and A35 is the small, flat back window of the earlier car – a transitional design feature between pre-war styles and the more open look of the later 1950s.

4. The A30 was one of the smallest cars in the world to have four doors. This side view shows the well-proportioned appearance of the four doors (AS4) model. It looks very much like a scaled-down A40, which was the manufacturers' intention.

5. The comparatively small (13 inch) wheels of the A30 help to make it look proportionately right. Depending on the body colour, the wing moulding strips either contrasted with (as here) or matched the paintwork.

6. Both front and rear doors on the four door cars had swivelling quarter-light windows; the front door windows opened on a 'balanced lift' sliding principle, whereas the rear door windows were fixed. The door hinges protruded slightly.

7. All the A30s, and the A35 commercials until April 1962, were fitted with semaphore indicators. These were mounted between the doors, on four door saloons, as shown here. On two door cars and vans, the indicators were mounted in the pillar immediately behind the doors.

8. A single stop/rear light unit was built into each rear wing on the A30, with the reflectors mounted on the rear panel. The rear bumpers wrap around the bodywork and, on all except the early (AS3) cars, are mounted behind a flat horizontal panel. Some have over-riders.

9. The bonnet handle was cleverly built into the attractive 'Flying A' motif on all A30s and A35s, although the badge bases on A35 models were longer, and made of zinc diecast material. This is an A30.

10. 'Torpedo' sidelights were a feature of all A30/35s. However the bases on the A30 were rubber (as shown), whereas those on the A35 had longer, metal mounts. Mounted on the wing tops, these lights can be seen from the driving seat.

11. The front bumpers wrap around the 'corners' and give good protection, being mounted on hefty irons. This A30 has over-riders, and the wing moulding strip contrasts with the surrounding paintwork. The front number plate hangs from the bumper bar.

12. The single jacking point on each sill serves for wheel-changing purposes only. Most cars now suffer from rust damage in this area, especially if the sills are still the originals – dodgy when jacking!

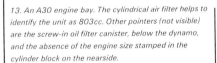

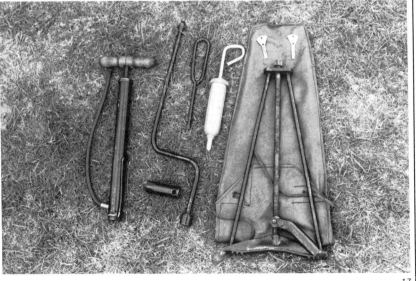

13. An A30 engine bay. The cylindrical air filter helps to identify the unit as 803cc. Other pointers (not visible) are the screw-in oil filter canister, below the dynamo, and the absence of the engine size stamped in the cylinder block on the nearside.

14. The passenger seat on A30s (even the four door variety) is double-jointed, to give easy, uncluttered access to the rear seats. The floor is free of obstructions which might trip passengers as they get in or out.

15. The front seat backs on the A30 are shaped to wrap around their occupants, and the seats have a soft, padded section at the front. Consequently they are generally felt to be more comfortable than the later A35 seats! Note the A30's long gear lever.

16. The rear window on the A30 is of course small by modern standards, and was enlarged with the advent of the A35. In most motoring situations this small window is not a handicap, and adds to the car's character.

17. By today's standards, the toolkit supplied with the A30 was extremely comprehensive with foot/hand pump, plug spanner, feeler gauges, starting handle/wheelbrace, screwdriver and jack being the main items. Unfortunately these have long since disappeared from most surviving cars.

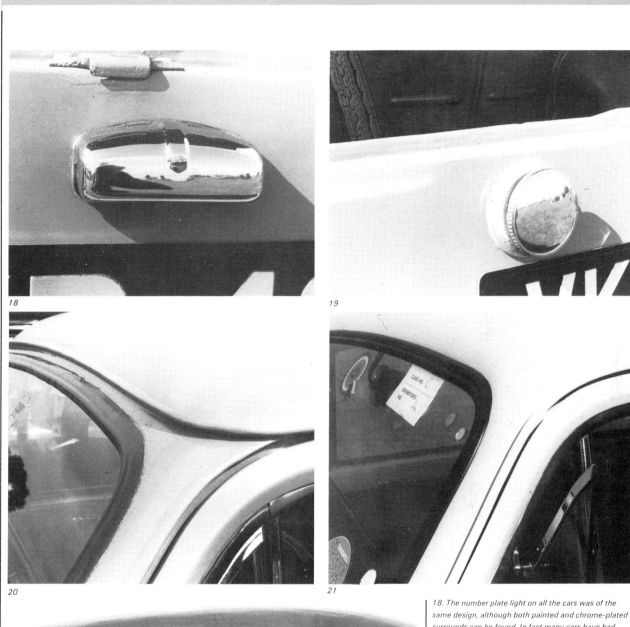

18. The number plate light on all the cars was of the same design, although both painted and chrome-plated surrounds can be found. In fact many cars have had their original painted units replaced by the chrome type.

19. Petrol caps, too, may be found in painted or plated form, and many cars have had locking caps fitted. All but the early (AS3) saloons have their fuel filler pipe let into the rear panel.

20. The roof drain channel on A30 models runs across the top of the windscreen, then back along the sides of the roof panel. However, on the A35 ...

21. ...Vive la difference! The channel turns down to follow the line of the windscreen pillars. This allows for a slightly more curved door profile at this point on the A35. Consequently A30 doors are not interchangeable with A35 units, as I discovered the hard way.

22. On two door cars the rear side window may be fixed in rubber, as here, or fitted with a hinged chrome surround. This option was (and still is!) a worthwhile aid to ventilation on hot days.

23

24

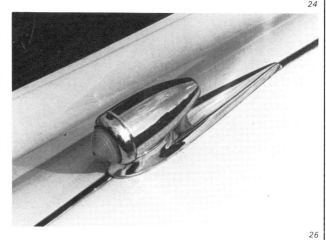

25

26

27

28

23. A35 rear wings have a different profile from the A30 variety, to accommodate the flashing indicator in addition to the stop/tail light. This was neatly achieved by incorporating a short, flat section in the rearmost edge.

24. The overall appearance of an A35 is neat, with the distinctive flowing body lines breaking up the fairly deep body sides. The wrap-around rear window of these later cars shows clearly here.

25. From the front, A35s are clearly distinguishable from A30s by their painted grille, with chrome surround, and by the flashing indicators set into the wing moulding line below the headlights. Small, but noticeable changes like these abound on the A35.

26. Another detail difference between the models was the use of a chrome-plated base for the sidelights on the A35. This results in a slightly sleeker look.

27. The larger back window of the A35 saloon gave the car a more light and airy appearance inside. From the outside, it retained a chubby, 'cheeky' look which gives it a lot of appeal today.

28. The 'Flying A' was still used on the A35, but the base is much longer than that found on A30s. Again, this helps to give the car a 'smoother' look.

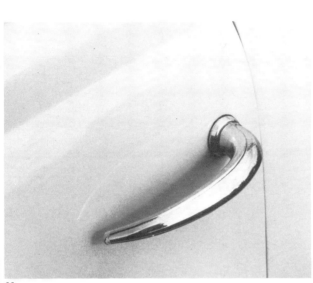

29

30

31

32

33

34

29. Door handles on all models were of this 'hook' design, and can droop a little as the mechanism wears, although this is easily rectified.

30. The flashing indicators on the front of A35 models are mounted on painted bases which convert the angled line of the front panel into a vertical attachment position.

31. Wherever you look on an A30 or A35, you will find

a clever combination of curves. Here, the sweeping, curved bonnet comes down to meet the rounded grille. All the lines seem to blend naturally.

32. The bonnet opening, however, is fairly narrow, particularly at the front. This, combined with the high wing line, makes for quite a stretch to reach some of the low-mounted engine bay components.

33. The compactness and comparatively

straightforward design of the A-Series engine means that there are no real difficulties in looking after it. The distributor is fairly low down, but all other regular maintenance items are easy to reach.

34. This view from the front gives an idea of how much room there is around the power unit. The battery and heater unit (where fitted) sit on the shelf at the back. Fresh air is fed to the heater via the trunking on the carburettor side of the engine bay.

35

36

37

38

39

40

41

36. Looking into a two door A35 saloon, from the driver's side; the most obvious difference from A30 models is the seating in the front. A35 seats tip from the front only – the backrest does not tilt, as in the A30.

37. The dashboard is simple and uncluttered, with a full-width parcel shelf below (all but AS3 A30 cars). Speedometers on the A30 vehicles were calibrated to 70mph, while those on the A35 are marked up to 80mph. The A35 gearlever (remote control) is shorter.

38. With indicator switch centrally positioned, the choke and starter controls flank the speedo, and switches for the heater, wipers, panel lights and ignition are housed below. Early A30s featured a round speedometer, with switches positioned around it.

39. The rear compartment is comfortable and cosy, with shaped seat panels for two people. For a small car, headroom and legroom is reasonable, although for tall passengers a few extra inches in each direction would be welcome.

40. Luggage accommodation is extremely good, and a family's holiday luggage can be packed in surprisingly easily. There is room behind the spare wheel for storing tools, spare parts, etc. The boot floor is flat over most of its area.

41. The curved lines continue round the back of the car, and the dome-shaped bootlid allows for the carriage of tall items in the boot. The boot hinges are external on all but the very earliest A30 saloons.

35. The horn is positioned on the driver's side of the engine bay (r.h.d. cars), as is the steering box. This engine compartment is particularly clean.

42

43

44

45

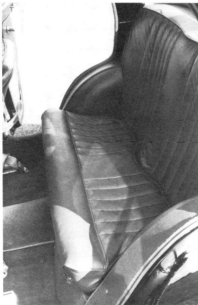

46

47

42. The four door A35 is an attractive little car, particularly suitable if a full complement of passengers is carried often. The styling is similar to the two door version, but perhaps better proportioned in appearance.

43. About a foot longer than the later BMC Minis, the A35 has much more of a 'big car' look about it. Nevertheless its modest overall dimensions make it easy to manoeuvre in traffic, and when parking.

44. Entry to front and rear compartments of the four door cars is straightforward, although the rear wheelarch intrudes quite a bit. This calls for care on the part of passengers getting in and out – particularly the not-so agile.

45. Rear seat legroom is good for a small car; the hollowed shape of the front seat backrest on the A35 gives more kneeroom than in an A30. The central propeller shaft tunnel is fairly deep on all A30s and A35s.

46. The siting of the rear seat immediately over the back axle means that the wheelarches must lie at each end of the seat. Although this restricts available seat width a little, the car remains comfortable for two rear seat passengers. The A30/35 is a true four-seater.

47. The rear doors, too, are shaped to overcome the intrusion of the rear wheels. The door trims are not elaborate, but tasteful, and match the colour of the seats. The door pulls on the A35 are chromed 'cups', whereas those on the A30 are pull-straps.

48. A popular accessory for the A35 was a steel sun visor, mounted externally. This has the additional benefit of keeping rain off the screen when the car is parked.

49. The A35 tool kit is comprehensive. All cars originally came with a driver's handbook, too. This is useful to have, as it contains a great deal of maintenance and general information.

50. The vehicle identification plate. In this case, the car is an A35 two door saloon, and the plate is mounted on the nearside front door pillar. This plate gives a lot of information about the car.

51. The A35 Countryman is the estate car version, and a very practical vehicle. Its 'boxy' styling makes it look rather van-like, but there are a number of important differences between it and the commercials.

52. Rather attractive fluted doors were used on the Countryman and the van models until 1962. This 'panelling' effect is also continued on the rear side panels, above the back wheels ...

48

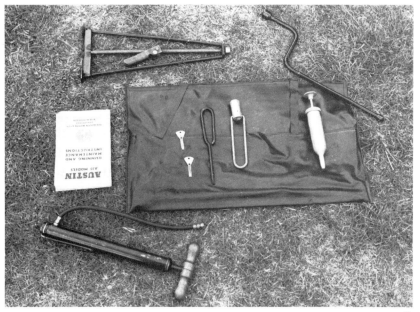

49

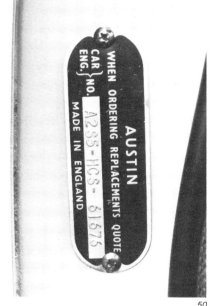

50

51

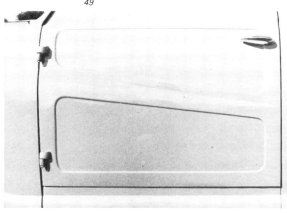

52

53

54

55

56

53. ...and, on the Countryman, sliding rear side windows are fitted in place of the plain metal panelwork of the van. The rounded wing line of the saloons is retained on the commercials and Countryman.

54. Both estate car and van versions have a single, wide-opening rear door for easy loading from the nearside. The Countryman has a rear seat as standard equipment, and, even with it in use, there is plenty of luggage room behind.

55. With the back seat folded, the Countryman has a long (almost 4ft 6in), flat load area, ideal for carrying large, bulky items. The rear compartment is upholstered, and a full roof lining fitted, in the estate cars.

56. The spare wheel is stowed below the rear decking, and is accessible without having to remove any luggage. There is plenty of room in the wheel compartment for storing tools, etc.

57

58

59

57. The A35 Pick-up is a very attractive vehicle, with a comfortable cab and a fairly small load platform behind. The flowing lines of this model are very different from the 'utility' styling of most commercials of the time.

58. With the spare wheel mounted on the rear panel, and with quarter-bumpers, the rear view of the Pick-up is totally different from any of the other models. A tonneau cover for the load area was part of the equipment.

59. An occasional rear seat was also provided by the manufacturers, with grab rails on the rear bodywork to help passengers when getting in or out. Alas, the comparatively small load area and high sides limited the car's usefulness as a pick-up truck.

60. A rear step was provided too, to help rear compartment passengers to clamber aboard. The A35 Pick-up was more useful as a personnel carrier than a true load-moving commercial. Even more it is an attractive 'coupe'.

60

61

62

63

61. *Many A35 vans, like this one, have been converted into estate cars by adding rear side windows and a back seat – kits were available to make this conversion. The result is a practical, comfortable vehicle.*

62. *One of the last A35 vans. Many of these were liveried, although most today are used for pleasure rather than business purposes. They remain, however, competent and hard-working load carriers. From 1962 the vans were fitted with saloon-type doors.*

63. *The vans were fitted with this vent in the centre of the roof; the Countryman was not so equipped, having a plain roof panel.*

64. *'Never raced or rallied!' Here a 1953 A30 is working hard in the 1954 MCC Lands End Trial. On AS3 cars, like this one, a winged badge was mounted above the grille, and the petrol filler was fitted in the offside rear wing. (The National Motor Museum, Beaulieu).*

65. *Another A30 (again an AS3) is being put through its paces here in the 1954 Plymouth Presidential Rally. The A30 and A35 were much rallied, in events ranging from local club affairs to famous winter dashes like the Monte Carlo Rally. (The National Motor Museum, Beaulieu).*

64

65

66

67

66. An A30 leads the pack through the chicane! The scene is at Goodwood, in 1956, and the car is an AS4 model. The nimble handling of the A30 offset advantages of sheer power held by the opposition. (LAT Photographic).

67. This A35 sent International endurance records tumbling in 1957 when it lapped Montlhery circuit (France) continuously for seven days and nights at almost 75mph! At the wheel here is Gyde Horrocks, leader of the team of Cambridge Undergraduates who organised the event. (National Motor Museum, Beaulieu).

68. Two A35s cornering hard at Silverstone in July, 1958. The second car, 69 PMT, is Graham Hill's famous A35 which he not only raced very successfully, but drove far and wide across Europe in addition to everyday use. (National Motor Museum, Beaulieu).

69. A line of A35s cornering at speed and giving the Ford 100Es a job to 'stay in touch'. This event was a support race of the 1959 British Grand Prix, but A35s can still be seen racing like this today, in the Classic Saloon Car events. (LAT Photographic).

70. The famous 'Flying A' led the way for nearly 577,000 A30s and A35s. That an estimated 20,000 survive after so many years is a tribute to their design, reliability, durability and popularity. Well done, Austin!

68

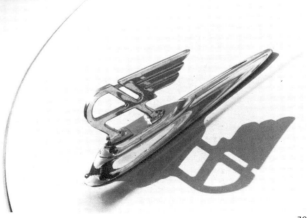

69

70

C1. This very original example of a four-door A30 is in
superb condition. An interesting point is the colour –
few cars in this attractive shade survive. AS4 models,
like this one, have a larger grille than the earlier AS3s.

C2. The same car shown from the side – the A30 is one
of the smallest cars ever to be fitted with four doors. The
family resemblance to the A40 Somerset and A70
Hereford models is striking.

C3. Of course, not everyone wants or needs four doors, and in recognition of this Austin offered the two-door A30 from late 1953. This particular car has appeared on television.

C4. From the rear the A30 looks quite 'upright', with the small back window emphasizing this aspect. This two-door (A2S4) is a good example of what a cared-for A30 should look like today,

C5. Even long-standing A30/A35 owners are surprised by the amount of luggage which the boot will swallow! Long-distance touring is no problem as a family's luggage is easily accommodated.

C3

C4

C5

C6. Optional on the two-door A30 (and later standard on the two-door A35 De Luxe), were hinged side windows to provide extra ventilation; bumper overriders; and twin ashtrays. Other options were hide upholstery (A30 only); radio; passenger sunvisor; and heater.

C7. The front end of an A35: curves in all directions! Again, this is Paul's 1959 car which has become his hobby. Although this car is only used in the summer months, many others are used as everyday vehicles, all year round.

C8. Paul Card's two-door (A2S5) A35 is immaculate, and has won many awards for its condition. However, the A30/A35 Owners' Club welcomes anyone with one of these vehicles – the state of the car is immaterial – and their enthusiasm has encouraged many rebuilds.

C6

C7

C8

C9

C10

C11

C12

C9. The extra door each side makes a marked difference to the car's appearance, although in other respects the two and four-door cars are identical. Interesting features are the contemporary wing mirrors and the shield over the driver's door window.

C10. The four-door A35 is comparatively rare, compared with the two-door variety. Black was a popular colour for A30 and A35 saloons throughout their production life. This car is the subject of a 'running restoration' at present, and the running gear is spotless.

C11. On later models, an addition to the rear light cluster was a flashing indicator.

C12. The chrome-plated grille on A30 models is surmounted by the attractive 'Austin' badge and, higher still, on the bonnet is the proud 'Flying A' motif. The grille badge on A35 models was slightly different.

C13. The A35 Countryman is compact yet very versatile. It will carry bulky loads when required, yet revert to a comfortable four-seater afterwards. This 1959 example has had some bodywork restoration carried out, to a very high standard, and is an extremely tidy vehicle.

C14. From the rear the Countryman and van models are very 'boxy' in appearance, yet retain a sense of style with the fluted panelwork and suggested wing lines. The fuel filler is recessed into the offside rear wing.

C14

C15. The rare and very pretty Pick-up. This one has been totally restored to its present 'as new' condition. As a pick-up truck is was not a success, but it is a much sought-after vehicle today.

C16. The red and grey contrast nicely in this rear view of the same vehicle. Of the 497 Pick-ups built, 250 were exported. Survivors are still being found around the world, but it is estimated that only about 50 remain in existence.

C17. The 'Austin of England' emblem appeared on the back of all models except the Pick-up. This says a lot about the confidence that the manufacturers had in their vehicles.

C15

C17

C16

C18. David Clark's Speedwell Blue A35 looks docile, but has Sprite running gear (including a 1275cc engine), front anti-roll bar and telescopic shock absorbers. It is therefore a fast road car, with handling to match its performance.

C19. The original A30 was referred to as the 'A30 Seven', and is depicted here on the cover of an early sales brochure. The new car was an attractive proposition, with many advanced features for its time.

C18

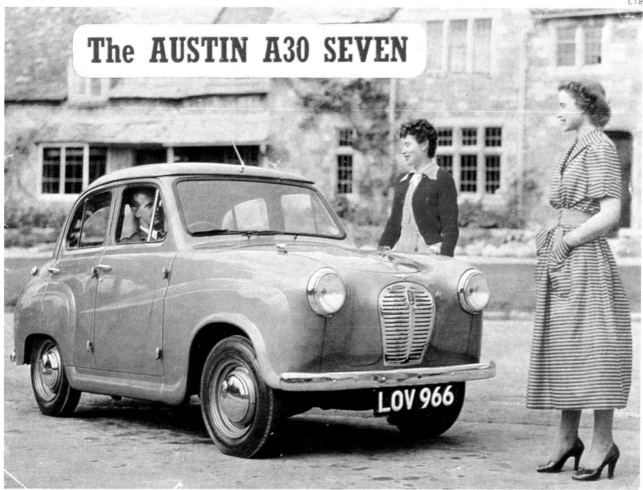

The AUSTIN A30 SEVEN

C19

C20. Austin were proud of the unitary design of the A30, and showed it off in their brochures with this excellent cut-away view of the car. The combination of 'maximum space within minimum dimensions' was a clever and significant achievement.

C21. Rust protection was important to Austin, and they emphasized this in their sales literature. That their efforts in this direction were largely successful is evidenced by the number of vehicles which survive today, many of which are as yet 'unrestored' and still in use.

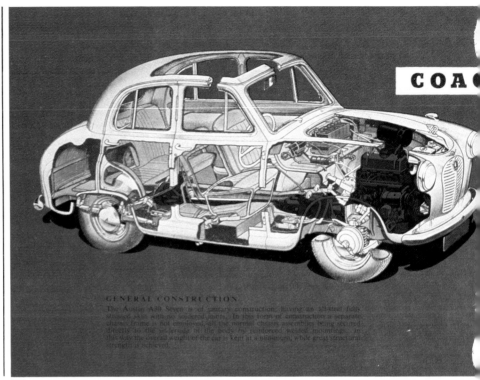

GENERAL CONSTRUCTION

The Austin A30 Seven is of unitary construction, having an all-steel fully stressed skin with no soldered joints. In this form of construction a separate chassis frame is not employed, all the normal chassis assemblies being secured directly to the underside of the body by reinforced welded mountings. In this way the overall weight of the car is kept at a minimum, while great structural strength is achieved.

C21   C20

Body Protection

ROTO-DIP

Before it is painted, each Austin body shell is placed on a revolving spit and sent through a 500-foot-long roto-dip plant. This in turn removes all grease from the metal, provides a phosphate coating to prevent corrosion and localize rusting following damage, applies a coat of primer paint and bakes the primer on to the body. The illustration shows a Seven body beginning its primer dip.

PAINTING

After treatment in the roto-dip, bodies are carried on moving conveyors through a vast paint-spraying system where the final priming coat and finishing colours are applied. The spraying booths are air-conditioned, surplus particles of paint dropping through the grilled floor to be carried away in constantly running water. Finally, the bodies are baked in ovens at a temperature of 240° F.-260° F. to give a lustrous, durable finish.